FEARED to Choose CHOSE TO Chance

Stepping Out when Fear Appears Instead of Taking a Chance in Not Doing

SHELIA HUMPHRIES

authorHOUSE®

AuthorHouse™
1663 Liberty Drive
Bloomington, IN 47403
www.authorhouse.com
Phone: 1 (800) 839-8640

Published by AuthorHouse 01/31/2020

ISBN: 978-1-7283-4398-3 (sc)
ISBN: 978-1-7283-4397-6 (e)

Library of Congress Control Number: 2020901361

Print information available on the last page.

Contents

Seize Each Opportunity

Frances J. Roberts, author of several books, literally captures your heart with her words that have been inspired by the Holy Spirit. In her book *Come Away My Beloved*, the pages seem to come alive as if God himself were there speaking directly into your life. An atmosphere of His presence unfolding hidden secrets that no one knew existed deep within you. It's like God reading your mail or the privacy of your heart.

Let the prophetic words from her message "Seize Each Opportunity" touch your heart. Clear your mind with a peace and everlasting desire to always be aware of the door that may be open before you with opportunity.

Behold, as the lilies of the field, and as the grass, so thy life is but for a season. Yea, though thou flourish in health, yet is thy time short. Thou hast no sure promise of tomorrow. Therefore, live each day as though it were thy last. **Seize each opportunity** knowing it may be the last.

For it is verily true that no situation presents itself twice the same. The opportunities of today are not those of tomorrow. Live not as though they might be repeated. Fail not to enter every open door. Be not held back by a feeling of un-readiness. I Myself am thy preparation.

For I will give to thee, the needed grace and wisdom for each moment as it cometh and thou shalt rejoice in the victory. For I will overcome timidity, and I Myself will displace inadequacy.

This is **My** work. I will do it Myself through thee if thou but allow thyself to be a channel for the flow of My Spirit. For I Myself am the life. I Myself am thy wisdom and thy strength, even as I am thy joy and thy peace. I am thy victory. My word is power because My word is spirit and truth.

Do not bear about needless burdens. They will but press upon thy spirit and interfere with My moving's. Much remains to be accomplished.

Linger not over what appears to be an unfinished case. Pass on. My Spirit will continue to strive though thou give no further thought. This way thy mind shall be kept free and thy path open, and it shall be ever a new way.

Keep ever moving, and from life to life I will accomplish My purpose. And know that as I work, all things work together, so that there is gathering strength and there shall be a glorious consummation. Praise God!

(Page 90)

Introduction

On the Sermon of the Mount in Matthew 7:24-27, Jesus tells us the parable of the two builders. *Those who hear* the words of Jesus *and does them* are likened to a wise man who built his house on the rock. Whether the winds came to blow the house down or the rains created floods that washed away everything; the house still stood and did not fall. But, for *those who heard* these words *but did not do them*, they are like the foolish man who built his house on the sand. When the rain came creating floods and the winds blew and beat upon the house, the house fell. And it was a great fall!

James tells us to be doers of the word and not just hearers; therefore, when hearing the word, action is required. When no action occurs or the response was in contrary to the word, the result is identical as the man in the parable. He heard but didn't do; therefore, his house was built on sandy unstable ground and when the rain and the storms came, his house fell, and it fell hard.

Many times, the people of God are unaware that a situation or circumstance in their life is connected to the destiny or plan that God has for them. So, they remain dormant when opportunities are presented and miss the step toward their destiny. Therefore, seizing the doors of opportunity with the right foundation is a must.

Chapter 1

Seize the Opportunity

. . . .

Webster's Dictionary defines the word *seize* as: *to take hold of suddenly or forcibly; to grasp, to grasp mentally; to take advantage of each moment; to understand clearly and completely, to seize an idea.*

As we read earlier in "Seize Each Opportunity," seeing and recognizing that the past is now behind and taking hold of or seizing the moment in front of us are important in our future steps. Paul states it very clearly in the third chapter of Philippians *"…but this one thing I do, forgetting those things which are behind, and reaching forth unto those things which are before." Verse 14 says "I press toward…"*

When we realize that we have been crucified with Christ and the old man has passed away, the past veil has been lifted from our eyes. Although, we may see clearer, many find it hard to recognize what is from God. Learning how to identify the Holy Spirit's direction comes when we spend time in the Word, and we become familiar with the Father's voice. Knowing who we are in Christ will enable us to forget about the movie of our past and the lies that the enemy keeps speaking in our ears. However, the enemy will continue to fire his best darts along our pathway hoping to create a giant of opposition and roadblocks that will delay us from our destiny. That's why Paul tells us to "press toward" the mark or vision that God has placed in our heart. I'm also reminded of Galatians 6:9 -- *"And let us not grow weary while doing good, for in due season we shall reap if we do not lose heart."* But do we always know that the situation or circumstance that we are facing is the very step that God has ordered in our life? I believe that God will show us through confirmation and/or a check in our spirit, when our eyes are focused on Him. Even though we live in a world of sin and we still live in an earthly body, the enemy is always going to try and redirect our eyes from the good toward the bad that will turn our focus on the situation instead of Christ. Jesus turns the bad into good, but we need to see the good in the bad. In the book of Job, we're told that **"what you have feared has come upon you."** When we become focused on things that may worry and /or discourage us, those "things" then have the opportunity to manifest or occur in our life. However, when our focus is on Christ, we know that no weapon formed against us shall prosper! When we press forward and refuse to give up on the journey and our eyes are clear from the "things" that are to distract us, we'll begin to see what God has prepared before us. Proverbs 23:7 tells us, *"As a man thinks in his heart, so is he."*

Seizing the moment can be difficult but when we take advantage of that time, we can say that we are taking advantage of an "opportunity" that has been given to us.

The word **Opportunity** means: *to take hold of suddenly or forcibly; a situation or condition favorable for attainment of a goal; a good position, chance, or prospect, as for success; "Opportunity knocks but once; seize a chance when it occurs or you may not get another."*

Being aware of the events within a day we would be amazed to see that life is full of possibilities. Every moment we're given an opportunity for something. We can open the door for a little old lady with her arms full of grocery bags or smile at the one whose head hangs low when walking the streets of loneliness or deep depression. We may have the opportunity to tell someone that Jesus loves them and has a plan for their life or to bless them with a bottle of water, etc. Life is full of open doors. But we must take captive or seize these moments that God gives us and do what is required at that time. Offer your assistance to the older woman or smile and tell someone that Jesus loves them and has a plan for their life. These opportunities are in front of our face; however, we don't see them because we're not looking for them.

Difficulties

"For a great and effective door has opened to me, and there are many adversaries."

(1 Corinthians 16:9)

Sometimes an opportunity is not always a blessing if you're not prepared to take advantage of that moment. God reminded me of a quote which says, ***"Every opportunity has difficulties and every difficulty has an opportunity."*** The challenges that one may face are the difficulties involved in the opportunity. The timing or the place where this opportunity occurs, the funds or whatever is needed for this task may be a struggle. Each opportunity has oppositions that seem to be mountains that are difficult to be destroyed and knocked down. But if we never give up or faint during the process, we'll see success.

Success may not always be the promotion that you wanted to receive in your job or seeing a project completed which has taken years to finish, but success is who you have become because of those things... realizing that you've become a better person because of this opportunity; you've completed the test despite its uncomfortable moments. Not giving up when the towel was right beside you to throw into the wind shows courage and determination to finish the race. When seeing God's fingerprints on each open door, we find that an encouragement of pressing toward that mark becomes the streams of living waters.

  ℰ *"Every opportunity has difficulties and every difficulty has an opportunity.* ℰ

It's wise to be prepared to face these issues before stepping through the door. When God says "go and do," there's no time for preparing for the journey. God is stretching your faith and trust in His word. And as

3

the Holy Spirit teaches and guides us through this process, dying to the self-will is an obedient step of humility and maturity.

So, what does the Bible teach us to do when the enemy attacks us through different oppositions that we face? In the Old Testament, the book of Ezekiel chapter 2:6 says, *"And you, son of man, do not be afraid of them nor be afraid of their words, though briers and thorns are with you and you dwell among scorpions; do not be afraid of their words or dismayed by their looks, though they are a rebellious house."*

The Prophet Ezekiel was told by God to go and speak to this rebellious house. As he stepped out to deliver the words of God, the people hardened their hearts, and rebelled refusing to hear what Ezekiel had to say. They were stubborn but knew that a Prophet had been among them. But in this verse, God was speaking to Ezekiel telling him how to respond to the oppositions and rejection that he received. This opportunity brought oppositions, but God still requested that His Words be spoken whether the people listened or not. God also said, **"Do not be rebellious like this rebellious house."** We are not to be brought down to the level of the enemy that places the oppositions in our life! But we are to be obedient in God's Word in order to fulfill the calling of the Lord. Therefore, we must die to the self-will that desires to launch out before God. The self-will proposes a possibility of sabotaging the plans for us and others.

The New Testament gives to us the directions on how to respond to oppositions that come our way. Luke 10:19 tells us that we can trample on serpents and scorpions and over all the power of the enemy, and nothing shall by any means harm us. Why? Jesus has given to us the authority to use His name because we are sons and daughters of the Most High God.

So, when we say, "In the Name of Jesus," because of the authority that Jesus has given to us, we can trample on serpents and scorpions and all the power of the enemy that tries to destroy God's plan. All through the Bible the Holy Spirit teaches us how to stand up against the oppositions that we face.

By speaking the Words of Christ and knowing He who lives within us is greater than he who is in the world, we are protected and shielded by the Blood of Jesus. Realizing who we are in Christ and that we were made in His image, lets us know that we are to be imitators of Christ and doers of his word, not just hearers. So, the Word tells us that love covers a multitude of sins and that we should love your enemies as your neighbor, as well as "turn the other cheek" and other verses that Christ has given us as our sword against the enemy. By being a doer of the Word and walking in the ways of Christ, our weapon is our Sword, the Word of God that we use to fight against Satan and his fiery darts. (Hebrews 4:12)

Let's look at three other verses in the Old and New Testament.

"Behold I have put My words in your mouth." (Jeremiah 1:9b)

In Jeremiah, the hand of God touched Jeremiah's mouth, anointing him with the words that he would speak forth to the nations. He feared the men within the conferences because of their harshness and evil hearts but God assured Jeremiah that He would take care of him and protect him. The light of God shone down onto the sin that reeked within the city walls with conviction. The people worshiped the works of their own hands, rebelled against God and burned incense to other gods. God's judgment was upon them if they did not repent and turn from their wicked ways. Because Jeremiah was a willing vessel to be used, when God presented this invitation to him, He assured this young man that his mouth would always be filled with His words to fight and destroy the enemy around him. (Jeremiah 1:8)

"This Book of the Law shall not depart from your mouth, but you shall meditate in it day and night, that you may observe to do according to all that is written in it. For then you will make your way prosperous, and then you will have good success." (Jeremiah 1:9b)

When Moses died, the responsibility was given to Joshua to lead the Israelites into the Promised Land. Just as God had lead Moses, He initiated the steps for Joshua. He let Joshua know that every place the sole of his feet would tread upon would be given to him, and that no man could stand against him; therefore, God told Joshua to be strong and of good courage for the Lord God goes with him. In this verse we are given 3 points on how to make your way prosperous and to have good success:

1. Never let the Word depart from your mouth
2. Meditate on the Word day and night
3. Observe (obey) it and do all according

"That if we confess with our mouth that Jesus is Lord, we shall be saved." (Romans 10:8-9)

Salvation, deliverance, power, and blessings are all wrapped up in our words. The Bible speaks of the importance of having God's Word in our heart. All of God's words are Yes and Amen; there is no negative in them. If there's power in the words that we speak, then God's Word is the sword that is sharper. Jeremiah's mouth was filled with the words of God because there's power and deliverance, love and forgiveness, salvation and rededication in them. When we confess with our mouths, we are speaking words that will bring the blessings of God. At the name of Jesus, when we speak His name, every knee will bow, and every tongue confess.

Many of the benefits and blessings of God's Word are not manifested in our life. Not having His Word hidden within us can be a hinderance when searching for the needed answer. However, when we meditate on His Word day and night, our Spirit fills with His Rama word. And when the enemy attacks, the Holy Spirit draws from within the camouflaged weapon, which becomes our sword for our warfare. Thus, as the words of God surface from our Spirit, we are now prepared to face any arrow that the enemy throws at us when confronted with difficult times. By standing on the Word that is concealed within, we force the enemy to flee when the Sword, the Word of God, comes forth with power.

The Opportunity that Matters

Opportunities knock at our door in several different ways but there's only one opportunity that matters. The Bible tells us in Matthew 6:19-21 *"Do not lay up for yourselves treasures on earth, where moth and rust destroy and where thieves break in and steal; but lay up for yourselves treasures in heaven, where neither moth nor rust destroys and where thieves do not break in and steal. For where your treasure is, there is your heart."*

All our riches and gold, possessions and assets here on this earth will not fit on the narrow road to heaven. Only "what we know that matters" will be accepted. Deuteronomy 30:19 tells us to choose life. Eternal life is the treasure in heaven that will never pass away.

> ℅ *Opportunities knock at our door in several different ways, but there's only one opportunity that matters.* ℅

When we take advantage of this opportunity that allows us to walk down that narrow road, nothing else will matter to us. We can now understand why the treasures here on this earth will be destroyed and will no longer be needed in the mansion prepared for our eternal life.

Mary and Joseph had left on their journey out of Jerusalem after spending several days there for the Feast of the Passover. After traveling a day's journey, they noticed that Jesus was not with them. Going back to Jerusalem, they found their son in the temple among the teachers. These men were fascinated with the boy's ability to teach with the knowledge of a man of age and wisdom. How did this young boy become so intelligent and how did He acquire so much wisdom? Even His parents were amazed and did not understand his behavior. After His mother had said to Him that they had sought Him anxiously, Jesus replied with these words:

"Why did you seek me? Did you not know that I must be about my Father's business?" (John 2:49)

Jesus knew that what mattered to Him, even at a young age, was to be a doer to what he heard his Papa saying. No matter the cost.

"I must work the works of Him who sent me while it is day; the night is coming when no one can work." (John 9:4)

When Jesus saw that the light of day was giving Him the opportunity to accomplish what His Father had requested of Him, He took advantage of that moment. His heart was to please His Father and to accomplish the task before Him because it mattered.

Paul and Luke put God and His kingdom first. The importance of obeying God rather than man was in their hearts.

"But Peter and the other apostles answered and said: 'We ought to obey God rather than men." (Acts 5:29)

"But seek ye first the kingdom of God and then all these things shall be added unto you." (Luke 12:31)

Paul took the opportunity to speak to the crowds when they became silent in Acts 21:40. They listened intently when Paul spoke in their native language. Even though Paul was able to stand up and defend himself, this opportunity of eternal life mattered. He did what was necessary to bring forth the message of life to those who had been blinded to the truth. So, to receive this eternal life that Paul spoke about, the people needed to step out and believe that this man named Jesus was the son of God and through Him, there was a forgiveness of sins. When making Jesus Lord of your life, you feel a desire to serve Him with a passion that starts to burn within. It doesn't matter how many academic labels we've earned, how many millions we've made, nor what we've stored up here on earth, nothing will fit on the narrow road to heaven except what matters. Now, being free to walk that narrow path, making Jesus Lord is the right decision that one can make. Because of our heart decision, nothing can hold us back from this eternal life that awaits us.

The disciples knew Jesus was the Messiah. When they made the decision to follow Him and obey His words, the enemy came to abort and destroy what they heard. But they continued to press forward with their desire to fulfill their destiny.

"Today if you hear His voice do not harden your hearts." (Hebrews 3:7)

"It doesn't matter what you know, if you don't know what matters."

All the abbreviations behind your name, the property that you own, all the assets you have, the business title you hold, the number of years of school or even the pulpit that you stand behind doesn't matter unless you have made **Jesus your Lord and Savior**. He should be "first" in your life. He is the only opportunity in life that matters!

Two Reasons for Opportunities

There are two reasons why Christ gives us opportunities in our life. The first is the chance to obey Him. The Bible has much to say about obedience. John 14:15 voices the words of Jesus: *"IF you love Me, you'll obey Me."* This verse gives an obvious reason for our obedience. Our love for Him. 1 Samuel 15:22 says, *"…behold, to obey is better than sacrifice."* This is merely telling us that obedience is better than anything. No matter how much we give up or lay down for the Lord, obedience is better.

Let me share with you two more powerful verses about obedience.

*"Now it shall come to pass, if you diligently **obey** the voice of the Lord your God, to observe carefully all His commandments which I command you today, that the Lord your God will set you on high above all nations of the earth. And all these blessings shall come upon you and overtake you, because you **obey** the voice of the Lord your God."* (Deuteronomy 28:1-2)

*"The Lord thunders at the head of his army; his forces are beyond numbers, and mighty are those who **obey** his command."* (Joel 2:11 NIV)

Notice the word "if" in the verse in Deuteronomy. As I said above, God gives us a chance to obey Him. God will never violate our **choice** or our will to make decisions in our life; therefore, this word "if" gives us an alternative to choose. "If" also gives the option to make a choice between side A or side B. When we know what side A holds as opposed to side B, the decision should be much easier to make. But is it?

"If" we fully obey the commands of the Lord, we will see the **blessings** of the Lord overtake us. Now, that's a good reason to obey Him! I want the blessings, but I want the power that comes with the package of obedience, also. Joel says that those who obey become mighty and strong in Him! That's an even better reason to obey. But it's sad to say that many people don't obey Him; they follow their flesh. Therefore, they miss out on receiving the blessings and the strength in the circumstances that weigh them down.

When we've made that decision to step out into obedience, the enemy is always waiting at the door to steal, kill and destroy the plans and blessings that are wrapped within our opportunity. When we realize that obedience is a weapon toward Satan and his demons, we start to obey God more. Satan is always trying to destroy by different oppositions and roadblocks that dam up the streams of living waters. But he can't do anything "if" we obey God's commands.

What if Jesus hadn't obeyed and done what His Father proposed to Him? Jesus had a choice in the option that His Father gave Him. He could have told his Father that He was not ready to end His life being crucified on a cross. But because of His love for His Father, He obeyed. Remember when He asked His Father, "If it be Thou will, let this cup pass from Me?" Since Jesus knew what was before Him, He was hoping that in some way He could get out of the contract, but the Father knew His son's heart and Jesus knew how much His daddy loved Him. Not only did Jesus want to please the heart of His Papa by being obedient to Him, He died because of His Love for All. That's why it "mattered" to Him to be obedient. He was giving us the opportunity to choose life in Him.

"If you love Me, keep My commandments." Mark 14:15

The second reason opportunities are given to us is to be used by Christ in a the "connection set-up" for another's salvation or destiny steps. It's nice to know that we have a Savior that knows what we need and how we need it. Jesus allows certain situations to happen in our life for a purpose. At the time we may not think so nor like and agree with what is going on, but if we trust Him and walk the pathway that He's leading us in, His reason will start to unfold with clarity. The valleys that occur or the people that appear may not seem to be connected to our destiny or anyone else's, but by trusting Him, we will soon learn of His purpose.

Have you ever noticed people with a certain type of character, attitude, disposition, etc. always seem to appear in your life? And when they do, you want to run and hide! They seem to "rub you the wrong way" or "push your buttons" to the point that you want to lose your Christianity for an hour or two and let them have it! Have you ever felt like that? Boy, I have. I've had to repent many times when I'm faced with these people. But Papa started showing me how these people were building my character to be like His. If everything and everybody were perfect, this kind of emotional discipline might may not be necessary to experience. However, Jesus placed them in our life for a reason.

The Uncomfortable Tools

As a young girl growing up, I always heard the phrase, "If it's not broken, don't fix it." But later in life, I realized that you can't fix what you don't know is broken. So how do we identify the broken areas in our life? The moment we gave our hearts to Jesus, the cry for change expressed itself with forgiveness. His heart jumped for joy. This was giving Him an open invitation to change us. However, the tools He uses to make those needed changes are not usually our choice. Think about it, if we chose our own methods to grow and mature, we would never see change! God has His own tools that dig deep to the roots of those issues needing to be plucked out, removed and gracefully changed for lasting results.

So how do we identify those areas that need to be changed? A good illustration to visualize is an onion being peeled layer by layer until you reach the center or core of the onion. God takes one area or emotion of our life to cleanse and reshape into His image. Galatians 5:22: *"But the Fruit of the Spirit is love, joy, peace, longsuffering, kindness, goodness, faithfulness, gentleness and self-control."* As God starts to expose the truth of our fleshly souls, we realize that we don't resemble Him at all. The light bulb of reality is revealed with conviction through His Love. Our cry is for change and His goal is for us to resemble Him. So, the journey of this process begins with the breaking of our flesh, which hurts. The carnal ways of the flesh have controlled the soul for many years; therefore, learning a new walk in life can be exasperating, exhausting, and sometimes lengthy as God begins to change the fruit of your flesh to the Fruit of His Spirit.

Maturity and growth are developed by the oppositions that are wrapped within the opportunities of life. At the beginning of this book, we saw how life is full of opportunities. Every person holds an opportunity with an opposition that will develop another's life, and ours. Let's look a little deeper in the meaning of this.

There are unpleasant, uncomfortable, unwelcomed people and events that appear in our life, which are part of the tool belt of God. These unlikable people are (sometimes) the mirror for us to see who we are. Our character of good and bad comes alive. You'll see that Jesus is the only one who shapes us in His image, and He uses these uncomfortable situations in our life to do so. He knows exactly how to peel away the layers of "self" to get to the original identity of who He created us to be.

Jesus uses many different props in our life. He knows exactly when He will utilize the "who" or "what" to get our attention. Also, He may maneuver you into the position to speak into someone's life a direction or confirmation. But how do we know we could be advantageous to God and how do we know when He will apply these methods for change? First, we must be attentive to the opportunities and the voice of the Holy Spirit directing us. Knowing our steps are ordered by the Lord, listening for that still small voice of directive words to step out, we may hear and see the opportunity that presents itself before us. I'm sure you've heard the phrase, "You can't walk on water until you get out of the boat" -- basically the same principle.

Many times, the direct word to go, is heard or not heard and the step of faith and obedience is still required. You find that this move creates an action from God to respond. The assignment begins to come alive with clarity. Finding the reason for the appearance in this person's life, if you have a heart for others, may prompt you to step out in obedience quicker than the first time. The reason why you spoke when you did or the words that were said could be a confirmation or a conviction that Jesus has attempted to express to that person.

Another scenario is a connection to a connection to a connection. I call this the "connection set-up." This is not hard to understand: how God uses people to connect you to someone who introduces you to another person, then joins you to the final person God desires you to meet. Yes, this stream of mutually known people is how God may use you in their destiny. You could connect this person to another that finally takes them to the designated place that God intended, if you stepped out at the appropriate time that God gave. If you never moved forward in this opportunity, you may have prolonged the destiny or the direction for you and this person. Remember, whenever God orchestrates a connection set-up, whatever type of tool that He uses, you are in the equation. Don't forget to be aware of what and how He wants to teach and instruct you in His direction for your destiny. However, if you avoid this step given to you, God is not limited in resources of willing people to be obedient to make the move. His plans will be completed no matter what.

ᑥ *You could be a connection to a connection to a connection...* ᑥ

The most important part of you playing a role in "the connection set up" in someone's life is that you may have been the key to their salvation, the opportunity that matters!

Chapter 2

Chance, Opportunity, and Choice

When we think about "life," we see that the size of this word is small but carries large historical stories. From the beginning of time life has had its bittersweet existence of growth. From the unlearned to the technology that continues to amaze and rattle our small "pea brain," we could say life has been interesting and challenging. Our daily walk is filled with life-giving opportunities that are packaged with the COC's (Chance, Opportunity, and Choice). The COC's have been in existence since the beginning of time, but have we really paid attention to their purpose and meaning? Let's look at each one of these words that might hold a little fear but also a step of opportunity buried within.

Chance

Although the word *chance* is described and used differently in the Old Testament than the New Testament, its meaning is the same. The word *"chance"* used in the Old Testament was "the casting of lots." This word is described as making difficult and significant decisions by drawing on the ground, choosing a straw from a stack or rolling dice to find out who or what it might land on. This was the people's way to know how God was speaking a direction or giving insight for the decision to be made.

The meaning of *chance* or "casting of lots" in the New Testament was the possibility of making the right decision by a gamble or risk.

Both are similar in meaning but different in the way the answers are unfolded and presented. Today we look at the word *chance* as an "accidental or unpredictable event ready to happen that wasn't prepared for" …like a risk or hazard when stepping out, not knowing what the "turn out" is going to be. Still, similar in its meaning.

We must realize that *"the race is not to the swift, nor the battle to the strong, nor bread to the wise, nor riches to men of understanding, nor favor to men of skill, time and **chance** happen to them all,"* according to *Ecclesiastes 9:11*. The Message Bible says it like this, ***"…Sooner or later bad luck hits us all."*** Seeing that life is not always fair to us, we all suffer and experience bad luck, unfavorable circumstances along with an omen of "in the wrong place at the wrong time."

Therefore, *chance* is the unknown and unpredictable mishaps that seem to have no assignable cause. They just happen! And if you're like me, this is not the way you want to live your life. I like to know what's about to happen so that I can prepare before bad things take full effect. However, there are times that we're caught off guard. As we know, "bad things do happen to good people."

Let's look at how *chance* or the "casting of lots" was used in the Old & New Testament.

"We cast lots among the priests, the Levites, and the people, for bringing the wood offering into the house of our God, according to our father's houses, at the appointed times of the year by year, to burn on the altar of the Lord our God as it is written in the Law." (Nehemiah 10:34 NKJV)

When the Levites *"cast lots,"* they may have drawn on the ground, drew straws or rolled dice to make a final decision of who in their family would gather the wood. Stepping out and taking the risk (of choosing the right person) was a chance they took which could have ended in defeat instead of victory. They took a *chance* in choosing a person, not knowing the outcome.

The crewmen of the ship that Jonah was on took a *chance* by *"casting lots"* to find out who or what was the reason the mighty storm had suddenly developed. The arrow landed on Jonah. This was correct and Jonah agreed to be thrown off the ship. (Jonah 1) This direction was inspired by God; therefore, all eyes were focused on the sign from heaven that would determine their next step to take.

"And they proposed two: Joseph called Barsabas, who was surnamed Justus, and Matthias. And they prayed and said, ' You O Lord, who know the hearts of all, show which of these two You have chosen to take part in this ministry and apostleship from which Judas by transgression fell, that he might go to his own place.' And they cast their lots, and then the lot fell on Matthias." (Acts 1:23 -26)

This occurrence of the casting of lots was the only time approved by God to happen in the New Testament. After Pentecost this method fell into a disfavor, since the ministry of the Holy Spirit now filled the hearts of the people. (Acts 2) As they were led and taught by the Holy Spirit, their understanding increased with their relationship with Jesus, the son of God. Now, seeing through the eyes of the Spirit of God, they learned that the words Jesus spoke when He walked with them brought a new meaning to their Christianity. Becoming aware of the differences of those who had not received this Pentecostal experience was a concern and caused a challenging urgency to spread the good news.

Today, as we think about those who have not received Christ as their personal Savior, we realize their life is a chance. Not knowing that The Holy Spirit will lead, guide and protect them, among the other promises in the Bible, causes their life to be a "hope" instead of surety. Eternal life is only given to those who ask Jesus to be their Lord and Savior; therefore, until this choice has been made, life is a chance that may bring decisions marked with confusion and devastation.

"Chance" without Christ can be coincidence or bad luck. A few scenarios: when you step out of your house, the awning may fall on your head or a tree near the front porch may be hit by lightning causing it to fall on top of you. Or when you take a quick trip to the store five minutes away, a drunk driver may run into you causing a wreck that could have been deadly. Crazy unexpected accidents can happen, leading to death or other critical injuries. Every single one of us lives a life of chance and anyone can experience these freak accidents.

Therefore, we take a risk or a gamble in life hoping that everything is going to be all right.

However, the unbeliever's life becomes uncertain when they turn down the opportunity to receive Christ as their Savior. And this "life taking chance" becomes that gamble when the unbeliever is not sure of the outcome. Like the "casting of lots."

The believer, the one who has made Jesus Lord of his life and depends on the Holy Spirit's leading, teaching, and protection has a knowledge that God is watching over him. The Holy Spirit is our comforter who gives us the security of knowing that we are in His hands. And when bad things do happen, the believer has a knowledge that everything is going to be all right even if it was a disaster.

"And we know that all things work together for good to those who love God, to those who are the called according to His purposes." (Rom 8:28)

Remember, the one who believes there is a God can still be an unbeliever! How? He may know of God but never have a relationship with Jesus. Having a relationship is spending time with Him by reading the Word. Obtaining the knowledge of the Word and fellowshipping with the Lord increases your faith and His Love for you, as well as your Love for Him. When you stand on that firm foundation, the circumstances and the sting of the enemy's attacks weaken because you know that Jesus holds all in His hands. His ways are not our ways nor are His thoughts our thoughts; therefore, our plans of the road to travel will be different than His. The Word tells us that His ways are higher than our ways! Therefore, when we choose to agree with His ways, He will agilely walk us though the storms and preparations ahead.

God never sets us up for failure, but always positions us for success. However, Christ is often accused of being the one who put this "bad stuff" on us. A good example of this is, **"Why didn't you protect me, Lord, from getting throat cancer or any other cancer?"** Jesus replies, **"Remember, when I told you to quit smoking and you didn't obey Me? Well, I didn't do this to you. You did it to yourself because you wouldn't obey Me, nor would you honor your body as the temple where I live!"** Wow, that cuts to the bone, but so true! Jesus delivered us and healed us from all sickness and disease and everything else when He died on the cross. We find ourselves blaming God for something that we're responsible for. We all take a *chance* when we step out of the will of God and refuse to walk in His ways. This opens the door to disaster or turmoil that the enemy tries to bring upon us, instead of the blessings that Christ has for us.

Chance Becomes Fear

When living this life of *chance*, not knowing what is going to happen next, a fear resides inside us. You may not realize it now, but it has a way of showing itself sooner or later.

There are many people who like to live their life on the edge. When taking a risk in a *"chance"* is activated, determination kicks in with fire for the unexpected to occur. In some incidents, that's a Russian Roulette game of life and death, to me. People take the risk of "Let's find out whether the gun has a bullet in it or not…" But, this stepping out and taking a *chance* can be converted into a risk of *opportunity* from God to accomplish the impossible. Having a fear to step out into the unknown becomes a paralyzing position.

If your gut feelings are saying you need to visit the church down the road, and you continue to remain where you are, then most likely fear is robbing you from an opportunity that awaits you. You're afraid to step out, and taking that chance has become a fear.

When an opportunity has been presented with confirmation stirring within us, the Holy Spirit may be trying to get our attention. The Word tells us that ***"Perfect love casts out fear";*** therefore, *chance* can now become an *opportunity*. When this door has opened, grace and wisdom are available to complete the assignment. In 2 Timothy 1:7 we see that God did not give us a spirit of fear. He gave us a spirit of power, love, and a sound mind. God equips us with strength and power to establish His Work. A sound mind that is positive of the call knows that God will prepare and supply all that is needed. No doubts and negative thoughts can confuse us when we are convinced it is God's request. Now, that fear has lost its grip, faith becomes the key that unlocks the door of opportunity for God's Work.

Hope & Faith

Let's look at the meaning of the word *hope*. The Webster's Dictionary says that *"hope"* is *the feeling that what is wanted can be had or that events will turn out well, to look forward to with desire and reasonable confidence.* So, for this favorable moment or opportune time from God, to have hope is to have an expected result. There's no doubt. But those who gamble, take risk, or chance, etc., may have hope but no expectancy of seeing the outcome. They can only wish for the best, as we discussed a few pages back.

Faith is not a negative word with fear wrapped around it. **"Faith is the substance of things hoped for..."** So, it is a decision that what we are expecting to see happen will come to fulfillment. However; *Chance* can be a negative and fearful word that's unsure of itself. So those who take *chances* are not making the statement that they believe, nor do they walk by faith. Their walk may be in fear, with a pessimistic outlook about the decision they've made. But those who walk in faith take a chance in stepping out and trusting God in the unknown or impossible tasks, by knowing and believing that the end results are positive.

So, when questions fill our mind with uncertainty or doubt, we need to examine our "knowing" instead of our "wishing" so that we can be ready to conquer the journey. Our hope lies within the faith of knowing instead of the negative side of unbelief. Everything is fighting against your hope of expectancy; therefore, you must see what you want, say what you want, and believe that what you've hoped for in faith is what you will receive!

*"**Now** hope does not disappoint, **because** the love of God has been poured out in our hearts by the Holy Spirit who was given to us."* (Romans 5:5)

Opportunity

"Opportunity knocks but once, seize a chance when it occurs, or you may not get another." Wow! I see this statement as a loaded time bomb. A chance of a lifetime, as they say. And it is! An opportunity that we'll never receive again in the same way, nor with the same people. An opportunity in a season of time that is full of everything that you need to succeed.

In the article, *Seize Each Opportunity* from **Frances J. Roberts,** we read that the Holy Spirit assures us that the grace and wisdom for each moment comes as we need it, so rejoice in the victory. Joshua 1: 9 admonishes us to, *"Be strong and of good courage; do not be afraid, nor be dismayed, for the Lord your God is with you wherever you go."* As we have already discussed in earlier chapters, the greatest opportunity is when you have accepted Jesus as your personal Savior. However, the Lord wants to give you other opportunities that He has chosen and designed for you. He has a specific assignment for you in His Kingdom, but we need to be alerted to the signs and the voice of the Holy Spirit that leads us in the direction of final victory.

If you recall one of the quotes given in an earlier chapter, ***"Every opportunity has difficulties and every difficulty has an opportunity,"*** you'll see that walking through to the other side is not an easy journey. Here are three points that we can expect Satan to use to destroy this possibility God has blessed us with.

Three Bullets That Destroy

Satan planned his attack on Eve with three points that brought that final fall. First, he questioned, second, he refuted and third he reinterpreted what God had said to her. The word *deception*, one of Satan's biggest tricks, can be defined as that which gives a false impression, whether by appearance, statement, or influence. Today, Satan continues to use these strategies in the lives of people through deception. So, let's look at each one of these bullets that the enemy shoots our way to kill the opportunity that we've been given.

The first bullet that the enemy fires at us is to *question*. Webster's Dictionary says that a question is an *inquiry, a reason or argument presented in opposition, a subject for debate and a feeling or expression of disapproval.* We are all given an opportunity that has a question wrapped around it. Why? The enemy wants us to ponder on our reason or reasons to cause us confusion and doubt. A question brings many thoughts needing clarity and confirmation, but the question presented can develop into a debate that enlarges deeper ambiguous feelings.

Satan, as we know, comes to steal, kill, and destroy, and his major tool is deception. The mind is the battlefield. This is where he deceives our hearts to believe the lie that he twisted to sound like the truth. He plays games with our thoughts by causing us to analyze the question until it becomes a ball of yarn. Our knowing that we heard from God becomes a question: "Was that really God saying that?" When he tears down our assurance to negative thoughts, Satan's dishonest ploy has started to kill the "call" with his poison of the deceptive question.

But there's another type of question we ask ourselves when God has presented an opportunity. "**Am I willing to pay the price with a committed heart?**" Receiving a request from God is an honor and is to be treated with high respect. At least I see it as an honor! Choosing me to carry out this plan for His Kingdom...I'm honored that my name was pulled from His assignment pot. But my questioning voice is like that of Moses: "I can't do this, I have this issue that cripples me". Right there we hear the questioning bullet from Satan himself who tries to replace our "I can" with "I can't"! However, Satan uses the reasonable self-examined question above also: "Am I willing to make this commitment and pay the price of the journey ahead in order to receive this victorious dream?" Ah!

Another key phrase that is embedded within the question is "my dream." Is this opportunity an answer to your dream that God placed in your heart? If so, then God will equip you with everything that is needed to fulfill your dream. Another reason why Satan tries to destroy is that he never wants to see your dream accomplished because he knows that it is God's heart and destiny for you.

Second, the bullet of *refute*. Webster's Dictionary says that refute means, *"to prove to be false by argument or evidence; prove wrong; to deny the accuracy or truth of."*

Satan kept speaking (a convincing argument by debate) into the ear of Eve that the apple was a good fruit regardless if God was telling her not to eat it. Satan told her to look at its beauty and its desirable taste. Knowing that apples are healthy and are good to eat, Satan asked her why would God disapprove of her eating something that would be nutritional and appetizing? Satan's deceptiveness was to convince Eve that the apple was good for her and wasn't going to harm her; therefore, his crafty temptation caused her to <u>disobey</u> God's word instead of trusting Him. Satan refuted the truth to make her disobey and to fall into his trap.

When an opportunity has been presented to us, the enemy immediately starts to twist the truth with lies and cunning remarks. His refuted words become twisted questions that steal the true word God has spoken within your heart. We've all heard of the "never and cannot," phrases: "I will never be able to do that...I cannot... I always fail...I never win.... everyone sees me as stupid; therefore, I will never be smart..." These words that we speak are self-sabotaging and kill our dream. It is Satan who implanted the destructive thoughts as his bait that causes the flesh to be magnetically connected. But the flip side of that coin is, I can do ALL things through Christ Jesus my Lord!

And finally, the third bullet is, he reinterprets why God told her not to partake of the apple. The enemy assured her that this opportunity to learn and understand good and evil would be an excellent step to take. After all, her eyes would be opened to so much more of life. This was a lie and a trick from Satan to convince her once again that having this knowledge of good and evil would increase her understanding of life.

In my own life, Satan has tried to convince me that choosing the desires of my heart, one being ministry, will <u>never</u> develop as it did years ago. You do not have the "free" time to devote yourself nor the money nor the youth and passion that you did early in your life. Listening to the fears of having to sacrifice and surrender all my time has made me think or ponder on the question: "Am I willing to pay the price of the commitment?" Satan can reinterpret the call upon our life into a lie and cause us to refuse or be fearful of making a hundred percent commitment.

Hopefully you can see how these three bullets are connected to Satan's attempts to kill our opportunities. And, you can understand why you've been confused with questions that have invaded your mind. The question that can bring confusion, the refute of the truth into a lie, and a reinterpretation that this "call" does not "fit" you or that the opportunity is not from God…these are twists from the enemy of what you know is the truth within your spirit. Satan is a liar, deceiver, and schemer that can destroy your destiny in a second… BUT God!

As we learn of the props that the enemy uses to destroy the *"choice"* or a "free will" in the decision that we make in the opportunity we're given, we are able to stand in what we know is truth.

> ℘ *The one "who knows" is not a "chance taker"*
> *who <u>hopes</u> and doubts.* ℘

Choice

Choice simply means to *"make a selection, decision and/or an option to pick."* Like *chance* is connected to *opportunity*, so is *choice*. All three work together. The outcome of the opportunity that you've been given will depend on how *chance* and *choice* are used. We will see this when we discuss the stories in the next chapter. First, let's look and see how this word was used in the Old Testament.

In 2 Sam 24:11-17 NIV we see that God gave David three options as a form of punishment for the sin that he committed which was pride. *"Choose one of them for Me to carry out against you."* God told David to make a *choice*.

In 1 Sam 16:1 NIV Samuel was sent by God to go and anoint the King of Israel. *"Go to Jesse's house and have his sons stand before you."* As they stood in line, God told Samuel there was another son; therefore, he rejected all that stood before him and asked if they had another brother. As this scrawny looking young boy approached his bothers, they laughed and spoke that he could never be king. But God *chose* this young boy named David because He had a reason for the *choice* that He made.

Even Lot in Gen 13:11 NIV made a *choice* of where to live. We've all been given the freedom to choose in hopes of making the right choice. The Bible shows us what will happen if we *choose* death over life. We are told to *choose* life according to the words spoken in Deuteronomy 30:19: *"...I have set before you life and death, blessings and cursing; therefore, choose life, that both of you and your descendants may live..."*

Judas Iscariot made the choice to have Jesus arrested for thirty pieces of silver and because of several bad *choices* that he made, he committed suicide. Matthew 27:3-5 NIV

We all have been given the freedom of choice, but does our choice always position us for the blessings of God? No. For when we choose to follow another path other than the steps of the Holy Spirit, the results can be devastating. God has given us a freedom of choice which He will never override. But He always gives us an opportunity to choose and make the right decision by seeking Him first.

Choice is a positive word that says what you want or what you've decided. I choose to be an overcomer because the Word says I am. I choose to step out and take a chance in trusting Him who has sent me. It's my choice to stand on the Word and be a radical believer. I have chosen to be a risk taker, knowing that God is protecting me from all harm. I choose to walk through my fears that try to hold me back from the destiny that God has for me. Why? Because I know what matters.

In one of Job's many conversations with the Lord, he spoke with a knowledge that God can do everything. (Job 42:2 NKJ) He was <u>sure</u> of God's plan and purpose, so he was at peace inside. He made his choice in God because he knew; he didn't question nor, was he unsure of his decision, even though Satan tried to confuse him with the three questions we discussed earlier. Hearing the voices in his head and from his friends, Job refused to allow those confused words to entrap him. He stood on what he knew deep in his heart.

Proverbs 29:25 NKJ says, *"The fear of man brings a snare, but whoever trusts in the Lord shall be safe."*

Second Corinthians 3:4-5 NKJ says, *"And we have such trust through Christ toward God. Not that we are sufficient of ourselves to think of anything as being from ourselves, but our sufficiency is from God."* When we have this kind of trust in God instead of ourselves or others, we can do all things through Him.

When we know the difference between chance and choice, the opportunity that comes our way should be easy to choose. When we know who is on our side, stepping out to the "unknown" is not a chance; it becomes a choice. Why? Because we know that the Holy Spirit is leading and guiding us along the pathway. Especially when God has ordered our steps and has called us. By faith we know that He is with us to the end. Our destiny is in His hands because He has planned our future for His kingdom.

Chapter 3

Favorable Moments

The men in the Old Testament were given an opportunity from God that not only changed their lives but would turn out to be an inspiration and encouragement for us today. As we investigate the lives of these men, we see that these amazing opportunities were favorable moments. Did they take a chance, or could it have been a choice, is a question that stirs the heart of many. Receiving this honorable request, these men were favored because of their heart, their passion, and openness to be a willing vessel. Knowing that these men would complete the assignment, God could trust that His "choice" would see His prophecy fulfilled.

Knowing the ending of these stories, let's take a journey and see how and why production was developed and what the finished results created. The destiny plan that God prepared for the development of these events was not the red-carpet ceremony. There was much opposition that each man faced as he stepped out in obedience.

A Wholehearted Faith

Moses was given an instruction from the Lord, for the land of Canaan, which God had given to the Israelites, to be explored in an expedition. Numbers 13 tells us that several men from each of the ancestral tribes were chosen and sent to inspect and report their findings. What were the people like? Were they strong or weak? Did the land have rich soil for crops or was it not good agricultural land? Did they live in camps or strongholds, and were there forests?

The spies began their expedition and reported back to Moses and Aaron describing what they had seen; their discovery was amazing. Large clusters of grapes hung from two poles that were carried by several men. An abundance of milk and honey was available along with the rich soil for growing crops and other produce needed. They saw many different tribes that were large and powerful. These tribes, the Jebusites, Amalekites, Hittes, Amorites and the descendants of the Anak tribe, were huge giants that made the spies look like grasshoppers. The Canaanites who lived near the sea and along the Jordan were also in the land.

Caleb, the son of Jephunneh from the tribe of Judah, knew that taking possession of this land wouldn't be a problem. He spoke up in faith believing that this step of opportunity was of God and could be accomplished with success. Therefore, Caleb spoke up and said, *"Let us go up at once and take possession of the land, we are able to overcome it."* The other men spoke negatively against Caleb's request because of what they encountered. A fear had suddenly struck their hearts and had paralyzed their enthusiasm to conquer this land.

The ten spies saw themselves as grasshoppers to the giants; however, Caleb didn't look at the opposition in front of him because of what he knew within. He knew that God was bigger and greater than those giants, so he stood on that FACT. Plus, God had told them to take the land as their own, so if God said to do it, it could be done. God prepared them with the necessary tools to complete the job. Because of having a relationship with God, they knew that this promise was from Him. Caleb saw this moment as an opportunity to be obedient and to watch God bless His people once again. Caleb knew:

"Greater is He who is in you, than he who is in the world." (1 John 4:4)

**℘ It doesn't matter what you know,
if you don't know what matters. ℘**

There were two things that were strong in Caleb's heart. First, Caleb knew who he was in his relationship to God, so he knew his position in the Kingdom of God. Second, Caleb had a "wholehearted faith" in the eyes of God, and he had a different spirit in him which developed a desire to follow Him fully. (Numbers 14:24) He was not doubled-minded; he was stable and secure in his belief, knowing God. So, when he acted in obedience to the request that God had given, it was a *choice* that was made instead of a *chance* taken. He <u>knew</u> that he would see the Promised Land; it wasn't a "maybe" -- it was a definite fact of seeing the Land of Canaan.

As the story of Caleb inspires us today, no matter the storm that roars in our life, we are overcomers in Him when we choose to follow Him with a "wholehearted faith."

The questions that puzzled the minds of the Israelites could have been:

1. Why would God place them in the midst of giants?
2. Why did He say they could conquer the land of Canaan?
3. Was this an opportunity for God to show that He was greater?
4. Why did God put them in a place where they felt defeated?
5. Was this a testing time of their faith?
6. Why do we have a fear and see ourselves as grasshoppers?

Yes, this was a time of testing their faith. When God allows us to be in a situation that is uncomfortable, it's for a reason. We can conquer that which He presents to us when we see that the Greater One lives within us. In the moment of panic, the attacks of the enemy look unbearable and unrealistic to overcome, but because of His perfect love, fear is cast out.

The Expected Flood

Noah lived in a world where there was violence and corruption. In the midst of this ungodly earth, he did not allow evil standards to rob him of his fellowship with God. Noah stood still on what he knew; therefore, God looked upon him to be a good man who found favor with Him. A "just man," and a "hero" of faith, a righteous man who obeyed God, were the descriptions behind his name. However, when God saw the wickedness that prevailed in the world, He was so angry that He told Noah His intentions to destroy the world. Noah was baffled to how God was going to do this, until He instructed him to build an ark. Not knowing what an ark was much less how to build it, Noah still knew that God was prepared to lay out the blueprint with the directions enclosed. A large boat that was to float upon water. Hmmm, they had never seen rain!

Noah followed every detailed instruction the Lord gave him. The construction company of "Noah and the Boys" took 120 years to complete building the ark. Noah continued to preach God's judgment and mercy to the world. He warned the ungodly of the doom that was about to unfold. Instead of listening, they made fun of him for building this boat when they had never seen rain. They called him a man out of his mind, and smirking laughs echoed while they gossiped about seeing the signs of insanity. But, little did they know, the finger pointed back at them and their ignorance deceived them with blinded eyes. However, Noah knew that the step he took was a true directive from the Lord. No doubt entered his mind; therefore, the darted oppositions fell to the ground with no life. He stood on what he knew in his heart because he knew what mattered.

When Noah was notified by God to build an Ark because He was going to destroy the world, an Expected Flood of uneasiness gripped Noah's heart. He didn't realize the Lord had singled him out amongst all and chosen him to accomplish His plan. Stepping out and trusting God was a big level of faith for this kind of occasion. But the fear that tried to overtake him could not stand. Like Caleb, he was a man of faith who trusted God wholeheartedly; therefore, he did not choose fear, but he chose to chance and trust his God!

The choice to obey God in this opportunity was an honor that required faith and endurance for the assignment to be completed. After boarding two of each animal, insect, etc. upon the Ark, Noah shut the door to a corruptive, sinful, and destructive world. By the hand of God, the water rose to a height that covered and destroyed all that was living. He created the rain to fall until the world was completely immersed and the ark began to float. When the rains stopped, Noah sent a dove out to look for land. When it returned with a green leaf in its beak, a rainbow covered the blue skies as a sign that new life had begun. Even though Noah sinned in several ways after this event, he became the first tiller and keeper of vineyards after the Flood.

ဢ *He did not choose fear,*
but he chose to chance and trust his God ဢ

Chosen Imperfectly

Moses received an assignment to deliver the Israelites and lead them to the Promised Land that God had given to Abraham, Isaac and Jacob. However, there was a conflict in the request from God. Moses knew God had chosen the wrong person to fulfill His petition; therefore, he argued with God. Having to go to Pharaoh and speak demanding words was an area that Moses felt insecure in. He pleaded with God to send someone else, but God *chose* him. Because Moses had a speech impediment or a stuttering disability, he knew that Pharaoh would laugh him right out the door. This embarrassment would cause him to shun future opportunities. Moses didn't want to take that *chance*. But God angrily told Moses that Aaron would speak, and he would perform the signs of the miracles before Pharaoh. Moses felt a little better about the new rules and agreed to the plan.

Prior to his trip to Egypt, Moses had seen an Egyptian man fighting a Hebrew man. Hoping a witness was not around, Moses killed the Egyptian to protect his native brother. Later in town, Moses was a bystander to two Hebrew men that were fighting each other which concerned him deeply. He tried to bring peace between them but recognizing that Moses was the one who killed the Egyptian, the men attacked him with these words: *"Who made you a prince and judge over us? Do you intend to kill me as you killed the Egyptian?"* (Exodus 2:13) Moses knew this event was known all over town; therefore, he feared for his life. So, Moses ran and hid and was skeptical of fulfilling God's request. Later, God assured him that the men who sought his life were dead and now he was safe going into Egypt.

Using this interruption, the enemy attempted to abort the opportunity that God had given to Moses. Trying to discourage Moses with his stuttering and the murder he felt convicted of was Satan's ploy to kill the opportunity Moses had received. But the heart of Moses was to obey and to honor God's command, so **"It didn't matter what he knew because he knew what mattered."** Moses and his brother Aaron traveled to Egypt. During their journey God was healing Moses of his speech disability, even though he was still fearful and unsure of his capability of speaking. When they arrived in Egypt and confronted Pharaoh, Aaron spoke the words that God gave him while Moses demonstrated the miracles.

Pharaoh rebelled even more after seeing the miracles and the signs that God showed to them. The heart of this Egyptian King was still unmoved and unchanged from his hardness; consequently, he punished the Israelites even more than before. Moses was troubled with this and questioned God of his role in this project. The purpose of this trip was to convince Pharaoh to let the Israelites go. But how was this possible if the Egyptian king punished these people more and pushed God's request away? As we know today from the Word of God, His ways are not our ways, nor His plans our plans. So, God knew that with a strong hand and these antagonizing events, the hardness of Pharaoh would soon break. And when God had finished with Pharaoh, the Egyptian king would be forced to let the Israelites go.

In Exodus 6:11, God spoke to Moses to go and *tell* Pharaoh to let the children of Israel go. Moses replied that the children of Israel had not heeded his voice, so why should Pharaoh heed him, *"For I am a man of uncircumcised lips."* God refused to hear those words from Moses because He spoke again to him in verse 29 saying, *"...Speak* to Pharaoh King of Egypt all that I say to you." Moses reminded God again that he was a man of uncircumcised lips: "How will Pharaoh heed to my words?"

In chapter 7 of Exodus, God approached Moses one more time, saying *"See, I have made you as God to Pharaoh and Aaron your brother shall be your prophet."* God chose Moses and made sure that he could accomplish the assignment. If Moses hadn't known that God thought he was worthy to do the job, he might never have done what he knew to do. That's why God kept telling Moses to go and speak to Pharaoh; He knew that Moses's healing had manifested and that he was able to carry out the assignment. **"We cannot do until we know but we can know and not do."**

The climax to this story is the seven plagues that invaded the life of Pharaoh and his people. Because Pharaoh's heart was hardened and unwilling to let the people of God go free, it took a devastating event to touch the heart of this man. However, God knew how to touch the tenderness within Pharaoh's heart. When God's only son, Jesus, was crucified on the cross, (even though God knew the outcome) He was hurt seeing the torture that Jesus went through. God's heart was crushed. God knew that if Pharaoh's only son was killed, his heart would be crushed to the point of letting the Israelites go. Consequently, the last plague that was sent from heaven upon Egypt was the Lord's Passover. The Lord passed through Egypt striking all the firstborn with death, but the blood of the lamb was placed over the doors of the houses where the Israelites were, keeping them safe. This was a sign for God to Passover.

After Pharaoh's son was killed and the people were let go, Moses led them on the journey to the Promised Land. Knowing the rest of the story and all the miracles that took place, we see how Moses encountered more opposition even to the end of his journey. The Egyptians followed them after the Passover in hopes to destroy them. When the Israelites came to the Red Sea, they saw a dead end. But God miraculously split this enormous sea in half, causing the waters to create walls on each side and allowing the Israelites to pass through on dry land. As the Israelites approached the far side, Pharaoh and his army entered the dry land hoping that the water didn't close its mouth. However, when all were in the depth of the sea, the walls of water were released and all of Pharaoh's army was killed.

It is an honor of trust that God has given us an opportunity to fulfill His Kingdom request. So why would you doubt Him in your journey? We can find many answers to that question but there's only one answer that fits. Fear. Although Moses was confronted with several oppositions, he stepped out and trusted that God was mindful of his needs and blessed him and the Israelites. Because God told him to do it, he knew that it could be done. But what if Moses had never placed his confidence in God and stepped forward in this journey, believing that his stuttering would limit his ministerial days? The story would still be completed but possibly in different ways and characters. The miracles and the supernatural events could have been performed at another time. God was going to get the job done regardless of who accepted the position. However, Moses may not have encountered God's miraculous healing and incredible miracles and future generations would have missed the supernatural prodigy of Biblical lessons and faith if he had never stepped forward and obeyed.

Moses didn't get to see the Promised Land because of disobedience; however, what mattered to him was to see the plan of God fulfilled. **"It didn't matter what he knew because he knew what mattered."** And that was to lead God's people out of the land of Egypt into the land that flowed with milk and honey.

The Man after My Own Heart

As we read of David being prepared for his blessing as King, his encouragement and inspired dedication instills in us a spiritual energy toward the journey of our destiny. Reading these Old Testament stories of the history and life of David and other great men of the Bible causes our faith to increase.

"...for the Lord does not see as man sees; for man looks at the outward appearance, but the Lord looks at the heart." (1 Samuel 16: 7)

When Samuel took his eyes off David's brothers and focused on David, he was astounded! When David, the little shepherd boy, was called by Samuel to stand in the lineup with his brothers for the anointing of "who is to be King of Israel," the heart of God spoke. Jealous, angry and outraged, the brothers watched Samuel anoint young, ruddy, bright-eyed and good-looking David to be King of Israel. God saw the heart of David. And God saw a man after His heart. So that day, the Spirit of the Lord came upon David to lead and guide him through the journey toward his destiny.

As soon as the ceremony was over, David went back to his job of being a shepherd boy. While he was in the fields waiting for the next step that would begin the journey, preparation procedures were in place. Can you imagine what was going through his head and his heart? Wow! David was by nature a very humble and patient boy, which was probably one reason why God chose him. Even when he encountered several giants that tried to destroy this adventure toward the throne of Israel, he trusted that God was going to help him fight his battles. And because of God, David soundly defeated the Lion, Bear and the giant Goliath. What an encouragement to keep going forward!

David chose to walk in a Godly fear that caused him to be obedient when he heard God speak. Not knowing what would transpire, he chose to trust God with a determination to complete the call upon his life. Probably unknown to others, David carried his secret weapon (a knowledge of God that we see long after his time in the New Testament) deep within his heart, walking with this verse on his lip: *"There is no fear in love; but perfect love casts out fear, because fear involves torment. But he who fears has not been made perfect in love."* (1John 4:18) David knew how much his Father loved him. Like the other men that we've discussed, God trusted him with a big assignment from heaven to complete, which was an honor. David knew that God would never give him this open door of opportunity to become King if His desire was to torment and bring disaster upon him. So, he trusted his Papa no matter what. **"It didn't matter what he knew because he knew what mattered."**

Let's look at the story of David and Saul and highlight some areas that should encourage us on our journey toward our destiny.

As a shepherd boy, David watched over his family's sheep, protecting them from wild creatures and animal theft. This bravery taught him to depend on the Lord and to fight. His character displayed the light of God within, and his good-looking physique and distinct voice were appealing in this young man. However, he understood that Israel was crying out for a leader and needed a King to judge them like the other nations and to fight their battles toward the Philistines.

Samuel, the Seer, was raised up during Israel's crisis. He was a transition figure between the era of the Judges and Kings. Samuel was Judge, Priest, Leader, Prophet and a Warrior, at an old age. He appointed his sons to rule and judge, in this time of "no king," which was approved by God. Many didn't understand why because their sins were well known. But God had another plan. The leaders in Israel saw that the sons of Samuel were disobedient and dishonest; they took bribes and had a perverted justice. Therefore, the leaders decided to take a new course in Israel's life, making their own decision for the man that would satisfy them as King. As Samuel prayed, the Lord spoke to him to heed the voice of the people. *"They have not rejected you; they have rejected Me"* (1 Samuel 8) So, God announced to Samuel that he would soon be introduced to a man who would be the choice of the people.

Saul, a young and handsome man, was seeking the seer to direct him to his father's donkeys that were lost. As their paths crossed and Samuel met him, God spoke and told him this was the man to be King of Israel. Samuel revealed everything to Saul that was on Saul's heart at that moment and Saul was shocked at his accuracy. Then the Words of God were spoken to Saul that he had been appointed to sit upon the throne as King of Israel. Uneasy in this decision, Samuel nevertheless submitted to God's direction to pour a flask of oil over Saul's head, anointing him to be commander of God's inheritance. After Samuel had secretly anointed him, and the word got out, many came forth speaking their concern about his ability as a leader. But Saul proved himself in small battles that he won, showing that he was capable to fulfill this position.

In the second year of Saul's Kingship over Israel, he chose three thousand men: two thousand for himself in Michmash of Bethel and a thousand for Jonathan (his son) in Gibeath of Benjamin. The rest were sent to their tents. Jonathan smote a garrison of the Philistines in Geba and Saul blew the trumpet for all of Israel to hear. When the Philistines heard about this, they prepared to fight Israel with thirty thousand chariots and six thousand horsemen. When the men of Israel saw that they were in danger, they ran and hid in caves, in thickets, in rocks, in holes, and in pits. (1 Samuel 13)

Saul and Samuel had agreed to meet in seven days in Gilgal, but Samuel was late in his arrival. So, Saul took it upon himself to have the burnt offering and peace offering brought to him. When he saw that the people were scattering and the Philistines were planning their attack, Saul was fearful. Because he saw the fear of the people, delaying the actions was not an option any longer. He violated this Holy War by offering sacrifices instead of obedience. After Saul had made these offerings, Samuel appeared and spoke, telling Saul he had done foolishly and had not kept the command of the Lord!

Because Saul was impatient and feared that the Philistines would come down on him in Gilgal, and Samuel didn't arrive on the planned day and time, Saul took it upon himself to make this decision. He did not keep the commandment of the Lord; therefore, his kingdom would not continue.

Saul continued to disobey God when he was commanded to go and destroy the Amalek tribe. Instead of destroying ALL, which was the command of the Lord, King Saul kept King Agag alive and also the best of the sheep, lambs and all that was good. He also set up a monument for himself. When Samuel heard of this, he was furious and spoke the word of God to Saul.

"When you were small in your own sight, were you not made the head of the tribes of Israel and the Lord anointed you King over Israel?" (1 Samuel 15:17 AMP)

In explanation of this verse, Samuel said to Saul that God was the one who caused him to have this promotion in the first place. He reminded him: when you saw that you were a small man of character and a nobody, God anointed you King over Israel. Why do you think that God would honor your decision when you went before Him and dishonored Him in disobedience? This was evil in the sight of God. Even though Saul obeyed God's command halfway, this was disobedience in the eyes of God. It's when we "fully" obey the commands of God that we see the Blessings of God. (James 1:7; Deuteronomy 28:1 NIV)

As the story goes on, we see King Saul still on the throne, but the anointing was taken away. Due to his rebellion and disobedience, the blessings of God had been removed. His pride in his Kingly position caused him to step out before God and do as he pleased instead of being obedient to Him. But as we know, God was preparing someone else to take Saul's place, the young man David.

During this time in Saul's leadership, he was determined to prove he was better than David. He was obsessed in captivating the hearts of the people by destroying the life of this young man he despised. His jealousy and envy caused him to be self-righteous and prideful instead of being obedient to God. But David remained silent and obeyed God.

Before David took his place on the throne, God watched how he treated the man that was eager to kill him. Having been faced with the opportunity to destroy Saul, David never laid a hand on God's anointed one. He respected and treated him with honor to the end. Again, we can see how David was walking in New Testament knowledge, not repaying evil for evil. The WWJD (what would Jesus do) bracelets were not around yet either, but I believe David's first question to God in the situation was: "What would you do, God?" David truly had a heart after God's heart because he <u>desired</u> to have the heart of God.

In David's journey, he knew what mattered. His salvation and being obedient to God were more important than proving that he was better. The Word of God says pride comes before a fall. Therefore, he humbled himself knowing he was nothing and that he needed God in his life. David unknowingly stood on the New Testament verse that God is greater than he who is in the world, bigger than any giant that he would encounter in life. But David also knew that **"you cannot do until you know, but you can know and not do."**

Because David knew God's voice, he could identify the enemy's tactful games of fear and lies. Satan tried to convince him he was not capable of being a king, nor would his destiny ever be fulfilled from God. However, every dart or weapon from the enemy that tried to hinder his walk got crushed to the ground. Because David "knew," the pathway before him was cleared and he was able to finish the journey.

God had His purpose in mind and gave David the opportunity to obey and complete those plans. But David had to **"do"** what he "knew" God was telling him to do!

> ℘ *"You cannot do until you know,*
> *but you can know and not do."* ℘

Unlike Saul, David's kingship over Israel lasted many years from 965 to 1005 BC. David was a man after God's heart. Even though David was a godly leader, he was still human with needs that caused him to sin. Because God brought forth God's son Jesus through the linage of David, the destiny and purpose for David's life was victorious. Even though David made his mistakes with sins that were uncalled for, like his affair with Bathsheba and the death of her husband, David still had a heart that God was looking for.

What if David had never stepped out to do what he knew to do? He trusted God in an opportunity that was going to take years to come to its manifestation. Depending on God to fight his battles with the lion, bear and Goliath and believing that Saul couldn't touch him nor harm him came from courage and dedication and trust. David took the word that God spoke into his heart that day when he was a shepherd boy and believed. His trusting God was made easier when he saw that this opportunity was an open door that would direct him to his destiny. **David <u>chose</u> to take this <u>opportunity</u> because of what he knew God had spoken to his heart.** *Chance* was not an option because of his trust in God and knowing who he was in Christ.

Many Are Called/Few Are Chosen

"For many are called, but few are chosen." (Matthew 22:14)

The voice of God stirred the heart of David when Samuel spoke the word of the Lord and anointed him with oil. Hearing a proclamation of a future that sounded "to good to be true" was exciting but scary. These words voiced by the seer himself, Samuel, gave promise to who David was in the eyes of God. For the Father to choose this young boy, knowing of the man he would become, announced the future for his life. (Jeremiah 29:11)

David realized the days ahead were not going to be easy. Dying to the old man allowed the character of God to be developed through cutting away the carnal ways and with testing times that would increase his faith and trust in God. David didn't question nor did he pester God with the "are we almost there" child-like question. Years went by but manifestation was being rooted in a new man that would take the position as the King of Israel.

A large picture, from David's calling and journey, outlines our future today. As David walked through this journey of preparation, these words spoke loudly within him: you are called, and you are chosen. In the stories of David and Saul, we see that Saul was called but not chosen by God. The people chose him. After his first year being King, his disobedience began to destroy the anointing upon his life. Alternately, David was chosen to enter the boot camp for this position early in his walk, but not until after the Spirit of the Lord had departed from Saul, did he take his place on the throne. God knew that Saul would not complete the call on his life; therefore, David was chosen and trained to be the King of Israel.

We're all called into the kingdom of God, but are we all chosen? No. As the verse in Matthew says above, "Many are called but few are chosen." Let's look at three main components God considers when seeking the vessel that will perform His Kingdom duties when chosen.

The Heart

The Old Testament heroes discussed in this book have shown a dedication from their **heart** to please and honor their Father's request. **They knew what mattered!** So, the first component God sees, knows, and hears is our **heart**. Everything we think, feel, and do is spoken through our heart. Proverbs 23:7 says, *"As a man thinketh in his heart, so is he."* After Israel was scattered amongst the countries, God soon gathered them back together, so He could give them the land of Israel. Let's look at how this verse reads.

"I, the Sovereign Lord, will gather you back from the nations where you are scattered, and I will give you the land of Israel once again. When the people return to their homeland, they will remove every trace of their detestable idol worship. And I will give them singleness of heart and put a new spirit within them. I will take away their heart of stone and give them tender hearts instead, so they will obey my laws and regulations." (Ezekiel 11: 17-19 The Open Bible)

God knows we may have the desire for a clean and contrite heart but also have the inability to make those corrections and changes accordingly. As our hearts have been scattered, misled, and controlled, and the decision made for Christ has become warped by the ungodliness that has tried to destroy it, there is a price to pay. Confessing our sins and repenting to never return and giving up the detestable idols and ungodly ways are required to purchase a new heart. Just as Ezekiel cried out for a new heart, we also can make our request known to God and He will be faithful to bring forth change for a Godly walk.

Having learned and seen through their accomplishments, the Old Testament men were solid in their commitment, dedication and their love to God. Accordingly, they had a heart to please the Father which led them to be **obedient** to His words.

Obedience

"If you love me, you'll obey my commandments." (John 14:15 Open Bible)

There are several incidents that explain the consequences to our disobedience in the Bible. Romans chapter 1 speaks of God's anger and wrath upon unrighteousness. The hearts of men that knew God were without excuse but refused to obey God. They did not honor nor glorify Him; therefore, He turned them over to their wicked hearts and a reprobate mind.

1 Samuel 15:22 says, *"It is better to obey than sacrifice."* You can sacrifice (or give up something) and not be in obedience. Although David's desire was to protect himself by fighting back when Saul was

trying to kill him, God gave an instruction to David not to lay a hand on Saul. David chose to obey God rather than to sacrifice the call upon his life. He could have killed Saul, but his opportunity to be King over Israel could have been denied by God. Disobeying and killing would have been for nothing.

The Biblical men we have discussed stepped out and trusted God in the opportunity that was presented to them. They listened and heard the command of the Lord and obeyed. Pleasing their God mattered! They were unaware that their courage and boldness to step forward and complete the task was a history- making event. What would the world be like if they hadn't obeyed?

Testing Times

The last point is the **testing times!** Remember when David killed the Lion and the Bear? When he defeated these deadly animals, he passed the test only to move to the next larger stone: Goliath, the giant who Saul and his army would not fight. David knew this was another opportunity to trust God to fight his battle.

The testing times are not fun nor pleasant to walk through. But they are necessary. The Bible tells us that through these testing times, character is developed, and spiritual maturity is conceived that gives birth to the ways of God. That is our heart, correct? To be more like Him? These times provide the cutting away of the flesh. As we catch a glimpse of the carnality of who we are, we'll want to allow Jesus to take the old and give us the new. Also, in these testing times, we have an opportunity to show our love, our faith and our trust in the Father while He shows His love for us.

From the beginning of time, God has tested man. When Adam and Eve were created, God tested the woman by telling her not to eat of the fruit of a certain tree in the garden. That request was about obedience to the voice of the Lord. Did she obey? No! In Genesis 22, God told Abraham to place his son on an altar that he had made. Abraham was asked to sacrifice his son by putting him to death on the altar, by fire for God. When God saw Abraham's obedience through this test, He provided another sacrifice, the Ram that was caught in the bush.

"But, O Lord of hosts, You who test the righteous, and see the mind and the heart. Let me see your vengeance on them; For I have pleaded my cause before them." (Jeremiah 20:12)

Testing allows the heart and the mind to be seen in true form. In Deuteronomy 8: 2, God teaches the Israelites by reminding them what He had done for them in the wilderness. This was to humble them and to test them, to know what was in their hearts. This showed Him if they would obey and keep His commandments. Throughout the Old Testament are many stories that show how the Israelites and others were tested.

ℰ *Testing brings obedience through a heart of love and sacrifice.* ℰ

As we know, the New Testament is the Old Testament revealed. The same lessons apply in the New Testament but with a different spin. Here's a few verses that add to our lessons of encouraging words and humbleness in the testing times.

"Study and be eager and do your utmost to present yourself to God approved (tested by trial), a workman who has no cause to be ashamed, correctly analyzing and accurately dividing [rightly handling and skillfully teaching] the Word of Truth." (2 Timothy 2:15 Amp)
"…do not think it strange concerning the fiery trial, which is to try you, as though some strange thing happened to you…" (1 Peter 4:12)
"…count it all joy when you fall into various trials, knowing that the testing of your faith produces patience. (James 1: 2)

Chosen by Components

As we discussed earlier, we can see how God looks at the heart, obedience, and the testing times as necessary requirements for the saints to have on their resume. If experience has not been established, the process of acquiring these components will begin. Just as the employer looks for certain job skills for the job, so does God. The good thing with God is that we're all hired. But whether we meet the requirements or not with God, the testing times will continue until we get it right. With this in mind, we are ALL called, but the flip side of this coin, is the chosen. What is the difference of those called and those chosen?

As a new-born Christian, we start with baby steps as we learn and grow. Our love toward Him dictates our desire to obey Him. But not everyone is willing to sacrifice their jobs, their family, their location, their friends or other things for God.

My opinion of "chosen" is one who takes the extra mile, the unheard-of command from God. The "chosen" are the ones whom God can rely on to take that extra mile when it doesn't seem possible. The "chosen" are the ones that won't give up and give in to the worldly ways. A "choice" is when you decided to do this particular thing, and "chosen" is when God chose YOU to do it and no one else. He picked you for this assignment. (We'll talk more on "choice" later.)

Please don't misunderstand me, everyone "called" can and will be used by God. God has a ministry for everyone. When "chosen," God has given you something that He wants to use in this assignment for His kingdom. Someone else can do the job, but He has chosen you because of a specialty within. Let's look at what the Bible says about the chosen people of God.

"You did not choose me, but I chose you..." (John 15:16)

Jesus chose the people of Israel as His special instruments to highlight His name in the world. The lessons and miracles that have blessed us and enlightened us in our journey, along with other reasons, have encouraged and matured us because of those wilderness days. Peter described the Christians as a "chosen generation" (1 Peter 2:4, 9) We are special in the eyes of God...the "apple of His eye."

The word "election" (1 Peter 1:1-2) comes from the Greek word, *eklegomai,* which means "to choose something for oneself." Other words are used to describe this special relationship that Christ has with certain individuals or groups, besides the words "the elect ones." Choose, predestinate, foreordain, determine and the call are words that indicate this special relationship where He has decided to fulfill His purpose within us.

A few examples: God chose David because his heart was like His. Noah was chosen to build the ark because of his faith and trust in God, even knowing the sky had never released a drop of rain. Moses was chosen because God knew that he would leave his family to fulfill the request of God and because of his heart for his people. Caleb was chosen to see the Promised Land because he had a "Wholehearted Faith" and knew that God was greater than any giant. God knows whom He can "choose" for His assignment to be fulfilled.

"When you come to the land which the Lord your God is giving you, and possess it and dwell in it, and say, 'I will set a king over me like all the nations that are around me,' 15 you shall set a king over you whom the Lord your God **chooses***; one from among your brethren you shall set as king over you; you may not set a foreigner over you, who is not your brother."* (Deuteronomy 17:14-15)

God knows who leaders are and those who are followers. Therefore, He has chosen some for governmental offices and some to teach or preach, etc. This area in our walk can be difficult. Many have a desire to be something other than the calling and the choice God has created for their life. However, there is a greater anointing when we choose to connect to His calling. That's why God has chosen us for His projects.

Chapter 4

Obedience Better Than Sacrifice

In 1974 the enemy had been playing games in my head. The year I graduated, 1975, I disobeyed God which trapped me in a rebellious walk into the world which took away twenty years of my life. November 4, 1994, I returned home to Jesus, determined not to let anything steal me away from my Lord again. I stayed with my parents for about four months and then moved into an apartment in April of 1995. A year later, my mother asked me to move back home and take care of her and my father. He had the beginning stages of Alzheimer and my mother had just found out she had mesothelioma, a lung cancer caused by asbestos.

Of course, I couldn't say no since I was the only daughter, and it was my responsibility more so than my brothers; nonetheless, it was hard to say yes! Why? I would have to give up *my* life to take care of them. My freedom, my furniture, and all the things that I loved would have to be packed away in boxes. Plus, I didn't know how long this was going to last. At the time I was in my late thirty's and ready to start a new life, making this step even harder to commit to.

Doing what was necessary for my parents at the time was a call that the Lord placed on my heart for that season in my life. I accepted this step of sacrifice with obedience, unaware that doors would open for ministry.

At my age, returning to the home I was raised in with my parents was hard. Living under their roof and following their rules and expectations was not an easy transition. But this time was different. My Father didn't have the voice of household authority anymore since the disease had attacked his body and mind. As a result, taking on the mother and father role was my responsibility now. As Jesus increased my ability to love with an unselfish heart, He also strengthened me to accept the things I could not change. It was hard to accept that the Alzheimer's disease was killing my father. After years of seeing him strong and manly, I now looked at a helpless and unfruitful man with a stolen life, and it broke my heart. In the past our relationship was not the best between a father and daughter, but Jesus took this time to heal my attitude toward him. We had butted heads and disagreed more than accepted each other's differences in those earlier days, but now that we desired to mend those disagreements, this disease had stolen our time. But God always turns the bad into good. Christ gave me an opportunity to share with my dad the Gospel, making sure that his heart was right with the Lord. A week after we had this conversation, he left us to take his place in heaven. Now he is free from the torture that the enemy used against his body and mind. My obedience was worth the sacrifice.

Many painful memories were resurrected that needed to be healed during my stay at their home. Now having the opportunity to put them to rest, confused and unpeaceful situations were ended. What a blessing! My mother and I had a good relationship except an invisible wall kept us from growing closer. At a young age, a trauma that I encountered caused me to "black out" most of my childhood days. Even today, I can't recall much of those early years. However, it was our spiritual differences that were deeply hidden that stole the bond between us. Root issues of fear, negativity, control and unworthiness in God's eyes were a few bondages that I observed. Being alerted to these emotions, I could allow the Lord to use me to share His word and, through prayer, watch miracles occur. By noticing the change in my life, my mother began to look at different areas in her life. Seeds were planted with a Godly conviction. Not that my life was perfect, but Christ used what I brought into the house, that was in my heart.

This happened not only in her life; Christ uncovered areas embedded deep within me that needed to be brought to the surface for healing. I stepped out and was obedient in the sacrifices that He asked me to walk in, that exposed the little girl that was still wounded. This awareness later brought total healing.

The walls that were intended to destroy the relationship between my mother and me were demolished. Restoring the union with both of my parents and know They are with Jesus brings me joy and comfort. God provided all that I needed for the ministry while a deeper healing was manifested in my life.

As I write this book, from the bottom of my heart I realize that I cherish each moment I spent with my parents in those nine years. It was a privilege and an honor that Jesus offered me this assignment: an opportunity to speak into my parents' lives through Christ while He ministered to me the healing that would bond my relationship with both my parents. I will never be able to share all that Jesus did in the depth of their hearts, but Christ knew and heard their cry. This opportunity for a deeper committed relationship with Jesus might not have been possible if I had not obeyed by sacrificing my life in this request. Jesus has a purpose when we obey Him.

Benefits

According to Webster Dictionary, the word *benefit* means *something that produces good or helpful results or effects or that promotes well-being; advantages; useful or profitable.* A good example is The Blood of Jesus Christ. As we partake of the blood sacrifice, we receive many benefits or blessings. There is healing, deliverance and power all in the blood. There is a protection or covering when we apply the blood to our life. After the blood was applied over the doors at Passover, the death plague that traveled through Egypt overlooked those doors and death did not enter. This is a benefit to why we would drink or partake of His blood. What the blood promotes is helpful with profitable results.

In the 14th chapter of John, Jesus taught the apostles, ***"If you love Me, you'll obey Me."*** Christ demonstrated His love for us by sacrificing His life on a cross. The benefit that we all received by Jesus obeying His Father is eternal life. (Philippians 2:8)

The goodness of God rewards us when our obedience occurs. And the ease of obeying Him is earned by our love for Him. Here are a few verses that encourage us to obey.

1. Obedience brings security (2 Kings 21:8)
2. To eat of the fruit of the land... (Isaiah 1:10)
3. Salvation (Hebrew 5:9)
4. All these blessings shall overtake you. (Deuteronomy 28)
5. Obedience brings blessings (Genesis 22:15)
6. Obedience bring righteousness (Romans 2:3)
7. Becoming mighty (Joel 2:11)
8. You walk in truth *(which is also a test)* (1John 2:4-6)

Many times, we are petitioned to do things while other times it is a demand. *"I beseech you therefore, brethren, by the mercies of God to present your bodies a living sacrifice, holy, acceptable to God, which is your reasonable service."* (Romans 12:1) In this verse we see a request but also a command. As a Christian, it is our service or duty to take care of God's temple. Whenever we die to our carnal ways to adopt the character of Christ or to respect His temple, there is a sacrifice. We set aside our agenda to be obedient to His will and His word in honor of our love for Him. These moments are not overlooked by our Lord. He sees all and He will bless accordingly, which is the benefit we receive. (Matthew 19:29)

Obedience & Sacrifice, an Opportunity

The story *"Seize the Opportunity"* (cited at the beginning of this book) says that opportunity is given to us for a reason. This window of opportunity may hold a key that unlocks or takes us to the next step of our destiny. If we miss this window, we can miss the blessings that God has prepared for this time. This window of opportunity is a time to obey. As we said earlier, God looks at the heart, our obedience and how we deal with the testing times. He knows our heart and sees our obedience and watches us in the testing times especially in the window of opportunity. A note of interest: the fire encountered within these windows is usually hotter and harder to walk through. Our carefulness as to how we respond and our attitude during these tests bring forth our obedience and faith.

When the woman asked Jesus if her two sons could sit next to Him in the kingdom, He asked if they were willing to drink from the cup that He was about to drink and be baptized as He is baptized? Hmmm… that's where many abandon the call.

The sacrifice or giving up something that we love positions us to step out and trust God. Our relationship is strengthened and rooted in a deeper ground from our adoration and faith than ever before. He sees the doer instead of those who hear only. Abraham was about to sacrifice the life of his son, regardless of the cost. God saw his obedience and willingness to trust His voice. As Abraham was about to lower the knife, God spoke and showed him the sacrifice in the thistles. A blessing was given to him from God that no other man had received. *"Blessing I will bless you, multiplying I will multiply your descendants as the stars of the heaven and as the sand which is on the seashore; and your descendants shall possess the gate of their enemies. In your seed ALL the nations of the earth shall be blessed, BECAUSE YOU OBEYED MY VOICE."* (Gen 22:17 NKJV)

Chapter 5

Fear to Choose, Choose to Chance

In Jonah's life, we see another opportunity placed at the fingertips of one who was chosen for the job. Jonah, the son of Amittai, ran from the calling of God into an area he had never dreamed of. He was suited for this job because he was from the Galilean region and the language and customs were familiar to him. Therefore, God did not allow him to escape his calling.

Jonah did not realize how serious this command from God was. Regardless of the evil and wickedness of Nineveh, God instructed him to go and preach repentance and judgment to the people. With many questions about God's heart toward the people, instead of obeying the Lord in His command, Jonah feared for his life and turned down the assignment. Jonah ran to the seashore of Joppa and found a ship leaving for Tarshish and took it. However, God didn't leave Jonah's decision unnoticed. Valuing his life, fearing what the people of Nineveh would do, Jonah ran from the call of God and that has its consequences.

As Jonah settled in the lower cabin of the ship, the crew, knowing he was down below asleep, managed the sail. The beginning of the trip was beautiful weather but then a sudden storm appeared with thunder, lightning and a wind that caused the ship to dip into the waves. The sea began to fill the ship until signs of sinking were evident. The crewmen started throwing off luggage and cargo, as they cried out to their gods, hoping to make the ship lighter to float. But nothing was working. What was the reason for these storms that suddenly appeared when they were not expected?

With urgency, the captain went to Jonah, waking him with a shout: "How can you sleep during this? Pray to your God!" Up on the deck, the crewmen agreed to "cast lots" to find out who was causing this trouble and why. The method of "casting lots" was used in finding out who had offended the gods that caused the storms. When the crewmen were cleared of the accusations, Jonah's name appeared for questioning. They demanded to know all about this intruder whom they did not know. When Jonah was interviewed, he knew in his heart he was the one who had invited this trouble. Hearing these concerns, Jonah spoke up and said, *I am a Hebrew; and I fear the Lord, the God of heaven, who made "the sea and the dry land."* (Jonah 1:9) Jonah admitted that he was running away from God, knowing he had disobeyed. The crew asked what they should do to stop the storm and Jonah answered, "Throw me into the sea and it will become calm."

Jonah saw the people of Nineveh as wicked. The act of *choosing* the *opportunity* that God had giving him was frightening; therefore, he wanted to see them destroyed and have nothing to do with helping them escape God's judgment. How God could have mercy and love toward this city was unbelievable to his heart. But because of God's heart of love toward them, an *opportunity* to repent and dedicate their lives to God was to be brought to them by Jonah. This assignment to speak the words of God that would give them this option to choose was something Jonah did not want. Consequently, he *chose* to take a *chance* in walking away from God's plan by refusing to do what he knew to do. So, he fled from the instruction that God had given him.

Jonah realized that he was the culprit and beseeched the crew to pick him up and throw him into the sea. He assured them they would see the skies clear to a beautiful blue with white fluffy clouds. That was a sure sign that he was the issue of the storm. Little did he know that God was about to sit down with him and have a talk. But where this conversation was to take place was not on the sandy beaches. However, God had it all worked out.

Treading water vigorously, Jonah felt pulled by an undertow seeming to grab at his legs. This suction was like a magnetic force, and it drew him into the mouth of this large fish. Deep in the belly of this fish (some say a whale), Jonah realized that his life was slipping away.

51

While wrapped in seaweed, a flashback of all the victories and blessings that he had received from God appeared before his eyes. "Will I ever see your Holy Temple; have I been cast out of your sight?" This was his shout that echoed in the belly of this enormous fish. The Lord heard his desperate cry and because of his affliction, He answered him. With great thankfulness, Jonah knew that his salvation came from the Lord. Worshipping the Lord, Jonah said that he would fulfill all his vows.

Jonah 2:9,10 *says: "…I will pay that that I vowed…" And the Lord spake unto the fish, and it vomited out Jonah upon the dry land."* (NKJV)

In this story, Jonah's eyes were on the "issue at hand" instead of God's heart. Seeing the wickedness of Nineveh and God's heart to save them angered him to the point of running from the command. His disobedience not only affected him, but it would have stolen from the people their blessing from God. Salvation, love, and forgiveness was God's heart toward this city, but He needed Jonah to deliver His word.

After the big fish spewed Jonah onto the land, the Lord spoke to Jonah a second time to go to Nineveh and preach the message of judgment and salvation. This time, Jonah obeyed. As the message was delivered, the eyes of the people and the King were opened to their sins. They were truly sorry and repented, prompting the king to make a decree. Everyone was required to wear sackcloth and pray to God and a city-wide fast was scheduled. When the Lord saw that they turned from their sins, He had mercy on them and did not allow destruction to come upon them.

Unfortunately, although the word spoken awakened their hearts and God had mercy upon them, they soon returned to their old ways. The city was destroyed about a hundred years after Jonah's visit.

Later in the story, Jonah's heart was not the heart of God'. His main concern was his own personal comfort which displayed as selfishness and a corrupted perspective on life. Jonah cared more for a plant that provided shade for his head than for God's plans, until God created a worm to come and eat the plant. God's concern is always on the spiritual value of a person's heart and life.

"It doesn't matter what you know, if you don't know what matters."

In conclusion to this story, the Lord commanded Jonah to go to Nineveh and preach judgment, but Jonah's first thoughts were about himself. Not realizing that he was ranking his pride first before God's will, Jonah allowed his fear of the wicked and evil among those people and his unwillingness to help in their needs, to cause him to take a *chance* and run from his calling. Noah, Moses, David, and Caleb stepped out in *fear* and believed regardless of the circumstances. History was established and lessons were taught throughout this allegory. Jonah's three days and three nights in the belly of the fish have been likened to Jesus' three days and three nights in the crust of the earth before He ascended to the Father. A death and resurrection appeared in both accounts.

Maybe you can remember an opportunity from Jesus when you have chosen to take a *chance* and go the opposite direction instead of taking a step away from *fear* into your blessing of destiny.

Chapter 6 ....

A Parable of Opportunity

....

The two quotes that were mentioned at the beginning of this book, **"It doesn't matter what you know if you don't know what matters"** and **"You cannot do until you know but you can know and not do"** are subconsciously lived out through our lives each day. Not knowing what is going to happen from day to day can cause us worry, anxiousness and fear and become a burden as we try to have all the pieces in the puzzle before its time. These feelings can also cause sickness and emotional handicaps that the enemy uses to destroy us. That's where trusting God comes in, knowing that God has the plans for our future already developed and ready to be manifested in our life. He patiently sits on His throne eager to pour them out to us.

Look at this verse in the Amplified Bible:

"And therefore, the Lord [earnestly] waits [expecting, looking and longing] to be gracious to you; and therefore, He lifts Himself up, that He may have mercy on you and show loving-kindness to you. For the Lord is a God of justice. Blessed (happy, fortunate, to be envied) are all those who [earnestly] wait for Him, who expect and look and long for Him [for His victory, His favor, His love, His peace, His joy, and His matchless, unbroken companionship]! (Isaiah 30:18)

In this verse, God shows His heart with anticipated love toward us! He **longs** to bless us, to heal us, to meet our needs and the desires of our heart. Knowing He's working behind the scenes in our life, we see the puzzle start to develop with meaning. A portrait of our unseen destiny awaits its final moment of appearance.

Until that moment, the anticipation builds with excitement. With the confidence of His love for us and His heart to bless us, stepping out and taking a chance in the opportunity speaks of a courage within us. A measure of fear may try to raise its head with a worry and uncertainty of the decision just made. But the choice to trust and obey Him and the sacrifice that's attached are worth the preparation and the victory in the end, confirming that He is waiting on us as well, expecting to survey our hearts in anticipation of victory: His love, peace, favor, joy and matchless unbroken companionship!

When we stand firm on the promises of God, we're standing in the assurance of His Word. We make a choice to trust and obey Him, knowing He would never guide us in a wrong direction. The enemy comes to steal, kill and destroy, not God! The steps of the righteous are ordered by the Lord, and the pathway is lit so we don't stumble. However, to hear Him whisper the instructions we need, we must fellowship with Him. He reserves the blueprints of the map that will lead us, while holding the keys that unlock the doors. But we must make a choice to follow His way instead of our way. Opportunities give us a chance to make a choice. But **we** choose who we will decide to follow.

Caleb had a wholehearted faith in God. Therefore, the chance that he took to go in and possess the Promised Land, regardless of the report of the Giants living there, was by the choice he made when he believed and trusted God. (Which quote applies here?)

"…Let us go up at once and take possession, for we are well able to overcome it." (Number 13:30)

Caleb's feet were planted on solid ground. Able to stand because of his relationship with God, he had a different spirit within. He followed the Lord wholeheartedly and faithfully; therefore, the Lord gave him this opportunity to conquer the land. (Numbers 14:24)

So, what was wrong with the ten spies? Their eyes were focused upon the giants in the land, which placed a fear within. Their belief and trust weakened in God; therefore, disbelief dominated their thoughts to the mental breakdown: "*I can't!*" They made the *choice* not to take the *chance* in this *opportunity* that God was giving to them. But Caleb saw this opportunity differently from the defeated mindset that they had. He saw the Promised Land.

Look at this parable that Jesus spoke which was an opportunity.

A Parable of the Great Supper

(Luke 14: 16-24 NKJV)

Then he said to him, "A certain man gave a great supper and invited many; and sent his servant at supper time to say to those who are invited, 'Come, for all things are now ready.'

But they all with one accord began to make excuses. The first said to him, 'I have bought a piece of ground, and I must go and see it. I ask you to have me excused.'

"And another said, 'I have bought five yokes of oxen, and I am going to test them. I ask you to have me excused.'

"Still another said, 'I have married a wife, and therefore, I cannot come.'
"So that servant came and reported these things to his master. Then the master of the house, being angry, said to his servant, 'Go out quickly into the streets and lanes of the city, and bring in here the poor and the maimed and the lame and the blind.'

"And the servant said, 'Master, it is done as you commanded, and still there is room.' "Then the master said to the servant, 'Go out into the highways and hedges, and compel them to come in, that my house may be filled, 'For I say to you that none of those men who were invited shall taste my supper.'"

In this parable, the Master giving this great supper announced there was no need to bring anything. All he wanted was their presence, but the three men he invited gave excuses why they could not attend. They didn't realize what they were refusing, and doors of opportunity were closed. Even when the Master said that everything was already prepared and all they needed to do was to come, they still made excuses.

"Reasons are how we got to where we are; excuses keep us there." Excuses will always keep us from taking the step into the opportunity that is before us. Excuses held these three men back from the opportunity given. Their eyes and concerns were focused on themselves instead of what the Master had prepared for them at the supper table. Their desires and needs were more important than obeying the Master. The reason we remain on the same step is the excuses made not to move forward. Hmm…sound familiar?

I'm sure that we've all had moments where our methods seemed better than God's. Even when our plan didn't work, we continued to disobey God's leading. With a desire to fulfill the call God has given to us, that hundred percent commitment to obey Him and trust Him is not in our sacrifice for Him. So, when an opportunity is presented to us, we are given a choice to step out and take a chance to trust His direction that leads to our destiny or the "connection set-up."

When God told Moses to "go," he didn't ask Him if the "to do list" was completed before he stepped out. He said GO. God had already completed the list with everything prepared for the assignment. The men we've been discussing stepped out and started the task given to them by the Father with no list, just faith. God's plan and method of preparing us is no different. The money needed, the place or facility that was needed, the materials that were needed and the workers were in place. Everything was at their fingertips. The needed props to complete your assignment are provided for you also. Even if this opportunity is the first of many steps, the blueprint is already designed, and the materials are provided, just not shipped to your front door, until it is time.

With each invitation of opportunity, God anoints you with Holy Spirit power to complete this call. Personally, I or all of us, need His anointing to be able to start and finish His request. So, this confirms that you can victoriously fulfill this opportunity. There's no excuse!

ঙ *"Reasons are how we got to where we are;*
excuses keep us there." ঙ

The day arrived when David was placed in Boot Camp for training. The book of Ecclesiastes tells us that there is a time and a season for everything. The interruption that bombarded David's life prepared and conditioned him to be a man, a warrior and a King; however, the day had not arrived for him to wear the crown. When an opportunity presents itself, at that time the window is open for you to accept the position. But the preparation or the training comes at another time as well as the assignment. As I shared earlier in the book, you are not the only one in this opportunity or kingdom assignment. The Father is busy preparing others that play a part in the scenes of your life.

In this parable, when the three men did not except the invitation to come to dinner, the master told his servant to go to the byways and highways to invite the lame, the crippled and the uneducated. The Master was looking for those that were hungry and willing to step out and leave their belongings behind to go and partake. These homeless and low-income type people didn't have anything to bring; therefore, the invitation was easy to accept. Nothing hindered their hearts from launching out into an unknown area of life; therefore, they had no excuse.

The Marriage Feast

Let's look at another parable that Jesus spoke that gave them an opportunity or invitation where everything was ready. This is the parable of the marriage feast in Matthew 22.

"The Kingdom of heaven is like a certain king who arranged a marriage for his son and sent out his servants to call those who were invited to the wedding; and they were not willing to come. Again, he sent out other servants, saying, 'Tell those who are invited, "See, I have prepared my dinner; my oxen and fatted cattle are killed, and all things are ready, Come to the wedding, but those that were invited made light of the invitation. One went to his farm, another to his business and the rest seized his servants, treated them spitefully, and killed them.

When the King heard about this, he was furious. He sent armies to destroy those who murdered and burned up their cities. Then he said to his servants, "The wedding is ready, but those who were invited were not worthy. Therefore, go into the highways, and as many as you find invite to the wedding.' So those servants went out into the highways and gathered together all whom they found, both bad and good. And the wedding hall was filled with guests. But when the King came in to see the guests, he saw a man there who did not have a wedding garment. So he said to him, 'Friend, how did you come in here without a wedding garment?' And he was speechless. Then the King said to the servants, 'Bind him hand and foot, take him away, and cast him into the outer darkness; there will be weeping and gnashing of teeth.' For many are called, but few are chosen."

Once again, an invitation was given when the King presented a wedding ceremony for his son. His servants were ordered to call for those who were invited but they refused. The King became angry and instructed the servants to go to the highways and gather all who would come. The wedding hall was filled with both good and bad people as his guests. However, when the King arrived and found one man not clothed in the wedding garment, he was furious. It was not requested of the guests to bring a food item; everything was prepared for them; however, to refuse to wear the wedding garment was an insult in the highest degree to the King. Wearing the wedding garment was a special mark of honor. These garments worn by royalty were given to those who they sought to honor. Sometimes, the garments were given out to the guests, but refusal to wear the clothing was not tolerated. Therefore, the King sent the insulting guest into prison to be tormented to pay for this crime. This is similarity of Christ. When one rejects Christ and never repents of his sins, eternal death awaits him.

Both parables gave an invitation that required nothing from the guests except to come. Those who were invited excused themselves because of personal affairs or they departed with foolishness. So, the Master and the King extended this request to those unlikely to accept this favored opportunity. Knowing that this was an honor, they freely and easily and fearlessly accepted with joy.

The opportunity presented to us in our journey is the same. It's easy and free to accept this offer from God; knowing everything has been prepared, we can fearlessly run to the call.

ᔈ *Come, for all things are now ready.* ᔈ

Doers not Hearers

James 1:22 says," *But be doers of the word, and not hearers only, deceiving yourselves."* Christ knows who appreciates the invitation or an opportunity that's presented to him. He doesn't allow excuses to dictate his heart. Knowing "what matters," in God's heart, he steps out and becomes a doer instead of a hearer. However, there are times when opportunity has been presented to us, but things have intercepted our will to step out and believe. Even though we did not heed the call, God hasn't given up on our desire to walk in that assignment. He continues to correct us by allowing us to re-take the test.

Opportunity will present itself again. However, the direction of how it appears and manner of character maybe different. When the door that opens in front of us is not seized, the blessings connected to that opportunity maybe lost. However, God always has plan B that will lead us to our future dreams, also. As Saul was disobeying the commands of God, David was being trained to step in and take over the throne. God has a vessel that is willing to step in and be a doer of His request, if you decide not to participate. So, it's wise to seize the opportunity when the door opens. Choosing to trust God in an "unknowing" opportunity can be the greatest blessing and reward in life.

Chapter 7

Don't Give the Devil...

"Your adversary the devil prowls around like a roaring lion, seeking someone to devour." (1 Peter 5:8)

This verse is given to us as a warning. This notification that the enemy is roaming around looking for someone to devour gives us an opportunity to watch, pray and clothe ourselves with the armor of God. In the beginning, Eve wasn't warned that a serpent in the garden was going to convince her to disobey. But she did receive a command from God not to eat of a certain tree there. God designed and created humanity with the ability to make a choice. God the Father, Jesus the Son and the Holy Spirit have always been gentlemen in giving to us the right to make a choice. However, the Word gives us the answers that we should choose in life. You have a choice between life or death; however, He tells us to choose life. Hints are scattered all through the Bible that uncover the answers that we seek. I like to look at the Bible as my answer book to the questions or the tests in my life. Life is an "open book" test and the Bible is our textbook.

When Lucifer realized that God saw his wickedness, his prideful and scheming ways to "remove God from His throne," he was kicked down to the earth and reduced to ashes. The war between good and evil began. Because of the introduction to "sin" in this world, a lifestyle was established that would not change until Jesus returns to the earth for His bride.

Lucifer, now named Satan, is the prince of darkness on earth. He is the father of lies and his purpose on this earth is to steal, kill and destroy. Using every tactic and scheme of poisonous darts and weapons, Satan roams this earth seeking the gullible, the hungry and the needy child of God. In order to kill, Satan uses the destitute emptiness of the gullible, needy Christian to deceive and trap him in a mindset of trusting everything and everybody except Christ. However, God has warned and prepared us through His Word how to defeat the enemy.

The day that you surrendered your life to the Lord, you became Satan's target. Hostility provokes Satan knowing you left your sinful past to have Christ in your heart. Your desire to be like Christ and to accomplish His will in your life prompted Satan to make a special attempt to destroy you. Believe it or not, Satan sees you and knows you. He knows your weaknesses, your lusts, your needs, your desires and your character. He's there with a demon to entice you in your weakness and tempt you with lustful thoughts. With practical needs, the enemy attacks our mind with ways to meet those needs that are not God's ways. Once again, when Satan sees that you have unmovable faith, and you're standing firm on the rock, he is threatened by you; therefore, he tries harder.

Satan is afraid when a believer knows who he or she is in Christ. As we stand on scripture and speak the Word as our sword against the enemy, he must flee. God is greater than he who is in the world. Not allowing doors to open and attack you, His blood will seal and protect you from his lies and deceptive schemes!

"The thief does not come except to steal and to kill and to destroy." (John 10:10)

"You are of your father the devil, and the desires of your father you want to do. He was a murderer from the beginning, and does not stand in the truth, because there is no truth in him. When he speaks a lie, he speaks from his own resources, for he is a liar and the father of it." (John 8:44)

Knowing the names that Satan is called opens our eyes to recognizing his attempts in our life and who he is to the world. The apostle John calls him the "father of lies" (John 8:44), Jesus called Satan the "ruler of the world" (John 12:31), Paul called Satan "the god of this world" (2 Cor 4:4); the "prince of the power of the air" (Eph 2:2); "the angel of the bottomless pit" (Rev 9:11); and the "adversary" (1 Peter 5:8). John in Revelation 12:10 calls Satan the "accuser of the brethren" which also shows us his persistence in his destruction toward God's people.

The second part of John 10:10 says Jesus came to give abundant life for those who would believe and trust in Him. But the enemy comes to block, hinder and tear down the avenues that God so freely gives.

So, what is it that we're not to give the devil? This scripture in Ephesians explains.

"Leave no {such} room or foothold for the devil {give no opportunity to him}." (Ephesians 4:27 Amp)

The Message Bible says, **"...Don't give the devil that kind of foothold in your life."**

Even though this verse is talking about anger in its meaning, the Amplified uses the word, opportunity. When we open the door of our heart, our thoughts, our ears and our mouth, without screening what we see and hear, words can be deceiving with an unseen destruction. Do you remember the old saying, "Give him an inch and he'll take a mile?" That's exactly what the enemy will do when we don't keep watch over the door of our ear gate, mouth gate, eye gate. He's out to kill and destroy God's plan for His children; therefore, we're in charge of not letting that happen.

So how do we do this? The more time we spend with Jesus, the more we receive of Him. His word becomes deeply embedded within our hearts and when the enemy strikes, we have our sword ready to use. The more we pray in our heavenly language, the more the spirit of God strengthens and prepares us, and the Holy Spirit will teach us, lead us and comfort us. When our cup is filled with His presence and His Word, the Holy Spirit now has an opportunity to quicken our spirit when things could be detrimental to us.

In these last days, I believe Jesus is opening doors of opportunity to prepare His end-time warriors. During those times, many battles, trials and teachings have been allowed by Jesus to equip us for the finality of this earthly life. Satan, knowing that his time of destruction is near, works overtime to cause God's people to give up by departing from the faith.

"Now the Spirit expressly says that in latter times some will depart from the faith, giving heed to deceiving spirits and doctrines of demons..." (1 Timothy 4:1)

Because of these oppositions that try to destroy and abort the opportunity to fulfill the destiny for our life and for His Kingdom, we must be aware and watchful. By keeping our mind and the door of our heart protected with the Blood of Jesus and His Word, we "don't give the devil..."an opportunity to come in and destroy.

Chapter 8

He goes With You

"When you go to battle against your enemies, and see horses and chariots and people more numerous than you, do not be afraid of them; for the Lord your God is with you, who brought you up from the land of Egypt." (Deuteronomy 20:1)

Remember when God brought you out of Egypt; the day you finally realized you needed a Savior and a Lord in your life? When everything you've done was highlighted on a billboard announcing that you were a sinner? Christ has a way of exposing who we really are to show us who we can become. Being vigilant not to believe the lies and the condemnation of the enemy, we must understand the love of Christ and the reason for His conviction. Our sins are thrown into the sea of forgiveness and He remembers them no more, but He uses these ungodly ways in our life to teach us His way.

"There, is therefore now, no condemnation to those who are in Christ Jesus, who do not walk according to the flesh, but according to the Spirit." (Romans 8:1)

After the veil has been removed and the truth is revealed, justification begins. Justification is the act of God (just as if we have never sinned) that has made us righteous (now we are in right-standing with God) and just in His eyes. Now partakers of Him who is righteous and has never sinned, He looks upon us in the same manner. Sanctification is the act of God that is conforming us in His image of holiness, which is a continual process. We are becoming holy. We have been cleansed from a sinful nature to a Godly and spiritual walk in the Lord. (Hebrew 10:14)

The mind is the battlefield and during this process of sanctification, Satan throws his darts of warfare. The enemy cringes when this walk begins. Never wanting to see the image of Christ within us mature and strengthen, he attacks with his best weapons and demons. When God delivered us out of our "hell" or Egypt, a transformation or renewal into the character of Christ needed to be done. It's alarming to know how much of the worldly ways have been adopted within our lives. A cleansing of the old to receive the new, sanctification starts the process of moving us into God's holiness. A process of change has already been designed by Christ but the obedience of doing His will is essential to discover the results of a changed life.

Realizing the giants we face are many and come in all different sizes and shapes, we must turn to God's Word which encourages us not to be discouraged and give up. Jesus speaks these words to us for a reason. If He brought you *out of Egypt*, then, God will *take Egypt out* of you. We fight not against flesh and blood, so knowing this battle is a spiritual battle, we must fight with spiritual tools. The Word tells us the battle is NOT ours but His and that He will fight our battles for us, but we are still responsible for our part. Warring angels are moved into the battle zone when we speak God's Word. Hearts are convicted when the Word, which is our sword, is spoken, and the enemy bows his knee at the mention of His name; Jesus and God's Word are sounded. The Word of God is our tool to use in the battles we face.

"...Do not be afraid nor dismayed because of this great multitude, for the battle is not yours, but God's." (2 Chronicles 20:15b)

God is fighting our battles for us and tells us not to worry or be afraid. But it would behoove you to learn the tricks and deceptive ways the enemy tries to open the door. Taking this responsibility to investigate where the door could have opened, teaches us. When we take inventory of what our focus is on, what we are speaking, what we watch on TV, and what we are hearing through others, we notice the open door. Because our ear gates, our eye gates and our mouth gate, were not protected, the pathway was cleared for the enemy to come inside. We must protect these openings that can give access to the enemy.

"And it shall be, when you hear a sound of marching in the tops of the mulberry trees, then you shall go out to battle, for God has gone out before you to strike the camp of the Philistines." (1Chronicles 14:15)

God has gone before you to strike down the enemy!!! What an encouraging word when facing the battles. The steps before you have been ordered by the Lord and when the Word of God is within you, you have your weapon, His sword. He's always with you! *"I will never leave nor forsake you."* (Hebrew 13:5)

Now Or Later

At the beginning of this book, we saw how *chance* is a word that is unpredictable. Considering its definition as a gamble or risk that is taken and an unknown element that has no assignable cause, *chance* is a negative word and so is *risk*. Having the same if not similar meanings, both words *chance* and *risk* must have "faith" as a primary receiver for them to receive positive feedback. Meaning, the possibility of receiving a good outcome or return in this investment of taking a chance or a risk in something will depend on the "faith" level of your expectancy.

The Biblical men that we discussed earlier had a faith level of expecting to receive what God had shown in the opportunities that He proposed to them. Even though a little fear accompanied stepping out and trusting God in the situations that seemed impossible to them, their faith in their God and knowing who they were in Him caused the impossible to become possible.

When the opportunity is ready according to what God has developed, maturity is not always completed in manifestation. Becoming spiritually responsible with Godly wisdom and clothed in Godly character are major steps that takes time to be developed. Allowing God to reshape and cultivate the land and the people for its developing stages requires patience. While God is working on these areas for the stage to be set, He has prepared several "tests" to restructure your walk and rebuild your character for greater strength and lasting stability. Preparation is necessary in these steps of your journey.

As God is developing each person connected to this puzzle, His desire is that everyone is complete and ready to enter in. You've heard the saying that God doesn't want you half baked; he wants you to be fully cooked and ready. This could be the reason why promotion for the next step is not offered and is delayed for a time. A good thing to remember is that delay is not denial.

And, another thing to remember is, **"Gifts can't take you where your character can."** You maybe gifted with many wonderful gifts like, singing, playing the piano or other musical talent, writing, speaking, or even dancing, etc. and be great in them, but have no character. The character of God is found in the fruits of His spirit: Love, joy, peace, longsuffering, kindness, goodness, faithfulness, gentleness and self-control. And we may think we walk in some, until Jesus shows us our fruit.

I remember when I was in the choir at a church I attended for several years. The music director and his wife were extremely talented. "He was very nice to me and always spoke, but she didn't. She had a beautiful Sandy Patty voice and I always tried to compliment her on the song she had sung, if I could get to her. This was a very large church, and on a few occasions would people get lost in the crowd. However, when I saw her, she never smiled at me nor acknowledged me when I tried to speak. Not that I idolized her, but her talent was up the scale in my heart. But when I attempted to speak to her, and I kept being ignored, my respect for her talent dropped down the scale. My first thoughts were that she did not walk in the character of God. I soon dismissed her as one of my favorite singers in the choir.

Sometimes, our gifts do take us out on the playing field, but we are half-cooked. And there are those whose character has been developed completely and then their fruit starts to rot. God knows when you're ready for the next steppingstone or for the curtain to go up, and it's time to perform what He has been preparing you for. So, during this process we've got to be patient. It might be now, or it could be later, God knows when it's the right time and you're ready to launch forward.

A good example is David. When he was given an opportunity to become King of Israel, he had to develop into the role of this strong warrior and leader that he was to be. He walked through many tests that were pruning him and shaping him to become the man of God; so that he could prove that he could not be moved when he was faced with the giants. But David had to walk through a season of time that required him to trust God and wait for the play to be fully developed before it was his time to perform.

In those early days, David had to step away from his comfort zone of being a shepherd boy to a place of believing and trusting God that required *faith*.

"Now faith is the substance of things hoped for, the evidence of things not seen." (Hebrews 11:1-2)

When David stepped out of his familiar and cozy position, he found that he had to make a choice which would require a risk or chance to be taken into an unknown area not yet visible. I see God anxiously wanting to show us what He can do for us, if we just let Him. But God's hands are tied when we don't step out of the boat and trust and believe in Him. We are grieving the Holy Spirit when we do this.

℘ **"Gifts can't take you were your character can."** ℘

When we don't believe and have faith that God can lead us in this opportunity that He has given to us, it is sin. *"...for whatever is not from faith is sin."* (Romans 14: 23b)

Since He gave you the opportunity, which is an honor to be appointed to carry out His plan for His kingdom, trust that He is going to lead you and guide you along every step. Remember? Everything is already ready. You just need to step out and trust Him and do your part.

Chapter 10

Serving Others

As we see in the story of Jonah, serving others was a prominent request. God's heart was to give these wicked and evil people of Nineveh an opportunity to know of His grace and love; however, He needed Jonah to deliver His word to them. So, the opportunity that was given to Jonah was not only for him but for others.

When conversion has taken place, God starts to transition your heart and desires from yours to His. However, the flesh will always put up a fight to hold on to the carnal ways in order to destroy God's plans. With this heart change in us, God starts to put new dreams and visions inside us, displaying His Kingdom purpose. An artist who drew and sketched worldly portraits now shares his heart in Heavenly and Angelic selections. A musical talent was transformed from a sacred sound to the spiritual heart of God. A desire to bless people through the gifts that Christ has given to you by sowing a seed into others has become a ministry within. A longing to serve others has become your heart. A Prophetic word that was given to me years ago was, "Dream Big." These words gripped my heart with excitement. Believing for the impossible in the Big Dream. Teaching and ministering to people have been a passion, and to see how God can enlarge this vision is exciting. If you have a desire to serve others through your talents or by teaching and ministering or by serving in a hospitable way, you have been summoned by the Holy Spirit. Because all things are possible in Christ, then, no dream is too big for God. Therefore, filling our heart with His dreams and visions causes us to believe for a higher expectation of manifestation.

Like Jell-O

Years ago, my heart was a cold, hard and unmovable stone. Feeling as though I had lost my identity, I was unsure of what I liked and disliked; therefore, I didn't like myself. The purpose for my life was camouflaged, making it hard to believe He had a reason for my existence. But night and daydreams captured my thoughts with unthinkable and impossible visions. The Holy Spirit reminded me of the Israelites who had a heart of stone. Ezekiel was told by God that He would give to them a new heart, a heart that was flexible and moveable. And with this new heart, there are new motives, flexibility and a new purpose. Encouraged by those words, I cried out to the Lord, asking Him to bless me with a new heart. Now able to see with a clear vision, I could "Dream Big" with a purpose in life that mattered. My heart became like flesh and moves like Jell-O, mobile and transformed to conquer the opportunities that He's prepared with a heart that can be moved.

Walking the path toward the "Big Dream" caused my heart to increase its desire to bless others. Celebrating one's salvation and seeing prayers answered is a joy. By being a vessel for God to use, you will see doors are opened for Him to utilize the gifts and the talents that He has bestowed upon you. Visualizing that the service we provide in our church or ministry is good; the unspoken and hidden requests in the opportunities given are priceless.

Double Set-Up

God likes to weave together dreams that connect. While you may think the opportunity is primarily for you, God is connecting others that have dreams and visions also. In an earlier chapter we talked about how the dots connect to one another. Meeting this person may connect you to another person and then to another, creating the "connection set-up" that leads to your destiny. When we seize these favorable moments, we may enter the "double set-up" helping each other to the next steppingstone.

Let's look at this scenario.

I had been looking for a gym to join with all the equipment and courts that I was seeking. I called a friend and asked if he knew of a gym, and he said he didn't but to call Tom. When I called Tom, he wasn't sure of a place but told me he had a friend that use to work at a gym. So, I called his friend and she said I needed to call Caren. I called Caren and she told me to go to Cook's gym and talk to Kelly.

When I arrived at the gym, Kelly was there to meet me. She gave me a tour of the gym and it was just what I was seeking. So, I joined. After a while, realizing that I was a Christian, she would ask questions about the gospel. When sharing with her, I realized that this was a God appointment. She invited Christ into her life which filled her with an inward peace she had been seeking. Kelly received what her heart had been searching for: Jesus Christ. And as time went on, I met a man who helped me with the ministry that God had placed on my heart, and he became my husband!

If I had not taken the opportunity of wanting to find a new gym, these events would have never happened in the way they did. This opportunity for Kelly was her moment to receive Christ. Could she have accepted the Lord later, somewhere else? Yes, but it wouldn't hold the blessings this moment had to offer. Could I meet the person to help me in ministry, somewhere else? Yes, but possibly not my future husband! This was a "connection set-up" which became a "double set-up."

It's easy to see why these moments are divine appointments from God. They were prearranged by God for us. Never knowing what each opportunity holds, can be crucial in a way when fear tries to grip us. That's why it's important to seize each moment. An opportunity may present a blessing in the moment or for our future.

But what happens if you don't take hold of the opportunity at hand? God always has a plan B on the side lines when His original plan doesn't work out; which means you're replaceable. Not a very encouraging word but it's true. Remember the three men that gave excuses not to go to the supper? The Master found someone else to bestow the blessings upon. And those that were willing were the ones that were unlikely to be chosen for the job. When Saul 's kingship was not working out, God had plan B: David, a young boy that looked like a weakling incapable of completing the task. God saw that his heart was like His; therefore, he was chosen.

The Biblical men that were mentioned earlier, were given opportunities that now speak to the hearts of many. When reading their stories in the Old Testament, we can relate to and associate much of our life today, just in different ways. But God had plan B on the side lines if these men had not responded to the call.

Now

The word *"moment"* is a *"now"* word. This word is not a future or past tense expression, but its meaning is *"this very second or an instant response."* So, to take advantage of the possibility is to seize the moment. The window of time can be crucial; therefore, stepping out in faith is necessary. When the first move is made, God begins to highlight the course of direction.

When the moment of opportunity is at our doorstep, we must capture this occasion before the enemy steals from us our blessing. If we miss it, God will give us another chance, but the same blessings that this moment holds will not be the same for the next time. As we discussed earlier, God always has plan B behind the next curtain ready to be opened.

Could the blessings, salvation and/or the call that Christ has upon the life of Christians be stolen when a moment of opportunity is not seized? It's a possibility. When a seed has been sown in times past, can it be watered when this opportunity is given? Yes. God will make sure that His people deliver His word to those who are hungry whether you accept the invitation or not. Because this opportunity was aborted (in our eyes), reaching our final destiny may be delayed.

True opportunity moments may not be the final runway for destiny to take off. But this moment of opportunity could be another step of preparation. When the true final runway for our destiny has arrived, an anointing with easy and flowing pathways is delivered and received. Therefore, when we beat ourselves up because we "feel" like we've missed this moment that holds our destiny, God maybe holding us back for more preparation.

When this opportune time presents itself, not knowing what it holds, we must seize the moment to know what is being served at the dinner banquet.

The Broken Ladders

At this time, I must elaborate on my journey in writing this book. When preparing this book, in reference for others, I was surprised to find that Jesus was talking to me. Climbing up the ladder of ministry (in one season) was successful, but I've encountered several opportunities that were not God. They were broken ladders.

Let me tell you the stories.

★★★★★★★

As I drove away from the church that I had attended for six years, God said He wanted me to start a ministry. Excited with a drive of passion I started to write the words He gave to me, but with questions. How, Lord, what do I do? The directions of the blueprint that He had already designed unfolded in my heart. I wrote the name of the ministry down as I drove on the interstate with a heavier foot than normal. Also, at that moment, I could feel the covering of the church lift from my body letting me know that I was released. I started to panic with a church nakedness until I could quickly join another body of Christ. However, the Lord reminded me that He was my covering, and His peace overtook my sudden attack of anxiousness.

Doors opened allowing me to connect with those who were there to help. Favor and blessings seemed to flow easily and quickly when

I reached for the tools or materials that I needed. Everything fell into place with an anointing of acceptance. Two and a half years went by and I had started to see that the ministry was slacking in attendance and open doors. It had always been my heart to go forward and do other things besides this one type of ministry. It is needed and I was still willing to continue but I wanted to do more.

A friend gave me the book *The Dream Maker* by Bruce Wilkinson. After the hundredth time of reading it, I knew what the Lord was saying to me. My heart was ready to leap forward and run toward that mark, but my mind had flashes of fear. However, through the book, the Lord would console my emotions with a picture of "the Big Dream." The more He allowed me to see, the stronger I became. Those fears started to fade into the darkness of night while the light of God brightened the pathway of destiny.

Tears continued to flow down my cheeks with the war inside. But my mind and heart finally agreed, and the final decision came forth. The ministry He had given to me so freely, I gave back to Him with an excitement. I handed off my torch to the one who would carry the fire. It was finally done.

★★★★★★★

The stages of the Alzheimer's disease that my father was diagnosed with rapidly developed, expediting the move to the nursing home earlier than expected. When my mother received the news that she had lung cancer, the Doctors gave her eighteen months to live. However, the Lord blessed her with nine years as opposed to the eighteen months that the Doctors diagnosed. Six years before my mother's transition to heaven, my father went to be with the Lord. Celebrating that my parents were free from the sickness that robed their life, I was blessed by Jesus for the sacrifice and obedient step of full-time caregiver in those nine years. I was blessed with my first home. After a year in my house, the Lord announced to me that it was "time to go."

As I continued to ponder on these words in church, I sensed an urgency to respond. Not knowing how to respond, I scheduled a meeting with my pastor. I had started attending this church when I moved into my house; therefore, I felt safe and trusted my Pastor's advice. I first met with his wife where her reply to the words that I had heard was, "Have you ever thought about going back to school?" I immediately said, "No" but when I met with my Pastor after church, he asked me the same thing. He convinced me to go to the College Weekend and make my decision then. I was excited about going but my gut feeling was telling me something different. I sought the voice of God for direction but again something didn't feel right to go, but I did. When I returned home, questions invaded my mind where I lingered too long for the answer. I missed the start of school; therefore, I didn't go at all.

During the next church service, the Pastor shared about some incidents that occurred at the church. A considerable amount of information could not be openly discussed; therefore, I was confused. But as I listened intently, I heard the answer to the phrase that echoed in my heart, "It's time to go." I heard the Lord say that it was time to leave the church. So, after I made my declaration to my ministry leaders, I left immediately. A week or two later, I asked a friend about the church. Her words shocked me when I heard that the Youth Pastor was put in jail for having sex with minors in the youth department. A Prophet and Prophetess (his wife was attending the church for a conference when all this was taking place) told me, "They hide the son (Youth Pastor) in another state from the police." It was soon exposed in the newspaper headlines, leaving the church congregation disappointed, embarrassed and with wounded hearts which divided the church. The Youth Pastor's father, the Senior Pastor, graduated from the school that he requested I visit on College Weekend. My Pastor wore his name proudly with much favor since he was an alumni and current teacher.

Before I learned of these events, I questioned the voice I heard in church: "It's time to leave the church." A confusion started to peek its head into my heart, and I started to punish myself for missing the opportunity. I had the money, the time, and the "Big Dream" to accompany. Examining the open door, everything looked right. I didn't lack for anything to go forward in school. But Jesus taught me a lesson during this time. He taught me how to listen to my heart and wait on Him to unwrap the gift and show me what's inside.

The flip side of the coin of opportunity is the "broken ladder." Not every opportunity is from God. Satan sets his traps to pull you into doors that are painted with all the colors you want to see. And his traps are to steal away the authentic mystery door from God. As I mentioned, some opportunities can be for preparation into our destiny, some hold the runway where destiny takes off, while another open door can be a trap of the enemy. Let me show you another "Big" false opportunity that I almost stepped into.

★★★★★★

As I stepped into this church, an excitement leaped within. Was this the church I was looking for? I was sure the answers that I had been searching for were nestled within the hearts of these people. There was dancing, shouting, prophesying, out-of-state guests with special performances and teaching from the Word of God. Intrigued and moved by this excitement, I carefully examined all that I saw and felt.

As I smiled and greeted those that passed by when the opportunity arose, I eagerly desired to be introduced to this fellowship. I received the new visitor greetings with the looks that followed which finally developed into conversation. However, there was an uneasiness that stirred in my spirit when I noticed ungodly characteristics. I kept an inquisitive eye on those of suspicion. Not sure of what the Lord was saying, I patiently watched. I soon made friends with those that affirmed my concerns, which was theirs also.

Probably impolite of me, I continued to stare with a pondering thought of "what is going on?" Actions among some were blatantly obvious that more deliverance was needed. Sometimes, in my prayer closet, I felt as if unspoken words of conversation were being transmitted through a familiar spirit. This wasn't right. Was I imagining these things or were they for real? A wall stood with no signs of crossing over to the other side. When unable to uncover their reasons or expectations needed for this cross-over, I did nothing at all. No-one would talk with me about what I was feeling or what they were expecting from me.

When I called to make an appointment with someone at the office, I never received a return call nor a kind word at church. I was rejected and ignored when I tried to politely acknowledge them. Nothing in return. Every door that opened I walked through with hopes of fellowship, but unspoken words said, "not interested." I made myself available at gatherings, but I received looks of, "what are you doing here."

The joy of the Lord and love for Him were expressed deeply in Praise and Worship but the characteristics of the Fruit of Spirit was never seen. (Matthew 7:15-20) My heart quickly responded to this opportunity that was not from God. Once again, it's time to go. Another broken ladder.

Chapter 11 . . . .

Commands of Love

. . . .

The love of God is an unconditional limitation of completeness, with no conditional terms of selfish interest in others. God is love; therefore, He shows no partiality toward people nor is He selfish. As one grows and develops in the ways of the Lord and obeys, he finds that God generously gives more of Himself. Proving ourselves worthy of the calling, as 2 Timothy 2:15 and Ephesians 4:1 portray, we find a secret for promotion is highlighted.

Commands of Love is an instructional step of becoming imitators of Him. *"Therefore, be imitators of God [copy Him and follow His example]. As well-beloved children [imitate their father]. And walk in love, [esteeming and delighting in one another] as Christ loved us and gave Himself up for us, a slain offering and sacrifice to God [for you, so that it became] a sweet fragrance."* (Ephesians 5:1-2 AMP)

Aware that the fruit of the Spirit does not reside within the flesh, becoming "doers" of His Word and of His character start to develop when one is obedient to the Word. When we stand on Psalms 32:8, the Holy Spirit extends His desire to teach and guide us in the way that we should go, counseling us as we become like Him. However, we must allow Him to work and move in our lives in His way, not ours.

Christ commands us to walk in the Fruit of His Spirit with Love being the first fruit listed. Galatians 5 lets us know that the works of the flesh are evident which is contrary to the ways of the Spirit of God. 2 Timothy says, *"He did not give us a spirit of fear but of love..."*, so there's no need to fear in God's words for our future. However, we do. Though the Word is written in our hearts, our flesh still tries to rule with uncontrolled emotions. As the tongue is a fire untamable in the course of nature, our love can be too. Just as the tongue can bless and curse becoming a deadly weapon to forcibly damages the heart, so can love. In the writing of 1 John 3:18, we are told not to love in word or in tongue but in deed and in truth. Therefore, our words are useless unless shown through actions.

"This is my commandment, that you love one another as I have loved you." (John 15:12)

Yielding

The word *yield* according to the American Heritage College Dictionary means to *give up; surrender or submit; to give up one's place.* For Christ to shape us, mold us, prepare us and perfect us to be ready to walk in His destiny, we must yield to Him, which means surrendering our *all to Him.* This gives Him the opportunity to work within our hearts. When we yield to Him, He can change us to His image of beauty and holiness. But how do we yield to Him? Through love! Because of our love for Him and His love for us, we're able to give ourselves unto Him. Although we see that Love is the key to all things, do we leave *love* out of the equation of our destiny? I believe that this does happen especially when a fear is buried deep within our soul. As 1 John 4:18 says, "There is no fear in love." So why do we fear? Well, this is and could be another book, but there are many reasons why a fear may be deep within our hearts. The fact is that fear or some other emotional chain has bound us from stepping out and trusting in His love. So, love is a part of the equation.

Loving Opportunities

"I delight greatly in the Lord; my soul rejoices in my God." (Isaiah 61:10 NIV)

The word *delight* in the American Heritage College Dictionary means to *please greatly, to give or take great pleasure and enjoyment in.* Spiritually speaking, we should find great pleasure in pleasing the Lord! So how is our Heavenly Father pleased? John 14:15 says, *"If you love me then you'll obey me."* Being a "doer" of His word is our desire to please and obey Him. Obedience is better than sacrifice. Not only does He desire to see us love and obey Him, it's His desire through the Holy Spirit to teach and guide us to become more like Him. However, the trials and tests of spiritual examination do not always exhibit a loving touch from our Heavenly Father. How could you…What are you doing…This doesn't make sense, are a few of the phrases commonly used in unexplained or uncalled for situations we encounter. By this time, we should know that there is a lesson in everything that happens. Look at this story.

★★★★★

*"On the same day when evening had come, He said to them, **'Let us crossover to the other side.'** Now when they had left the multitude, they took Him along in the boat as He was. And other little boats were also with Him. And a great windstorm arose, and the waves beat into the boat, so that it was already filling. But He was in the stern, asleep on a pillow. And they awoke Him and said to Him, 'Teacher, do You not care that we are perishing?' Then He arose and rebuked the wind, and said to the sea, **'Peace, be still!'** And the wind ceased and there was a great calm. But He said to them, **'Why are you so fearful? How is it that you have no faith?'** And they feared exceedingly, and said to one another, 'Who can this be, that even the wind and the sea obey Him!'* (Mark 4:35-41 NKJ)

Powerful words were spoken in this story. The first phrase that Jesus spoke to them was, **"Let us go to the other side."** He was making a statement of what was **going** to happen and when He says something, it will happen. So, the disciples **were** going to the other side. But when the storm came upon them, they weren't sure, so they started to doubt and worry. Seeing that the boat filling up with water and they saw their Master **sleeping** at the stern of the boat, they started to panic with fear.

This is a good word of encouragement for when Jesus gives us an opportunity. If He has given us the possibility to go to the other side, than He will take us there, regardless if the storms are raging. Storms do help us to grow; they're not all bad for us, but in our perception, we may see Jesus sleeping in the midst of our toiling. However, all we have to do is call out, and He will command peace to calm the raging sea. So now you can relax with peace and joy knowing that He is going to protect you as you go to the other side.

The three major points that we must see in an opportunity that has been offered to us are: *One,* **everything has been prepared for you in this opportunity.** *Two,* **you are going to the other side and the Third is, obedience.** If everything has been prepared for you to go to the other side, then why do you fear? If you have received His love, then His perfect love would never lead you somewhere unsafe nor unfitting in His plan for your life. In fact, His perfect Love cast out fear! And lastly, you'll never see the fruit of this opportunity unless you step out of the boat and **obey.**

> ℰ **Everything has been prepared & you are going to the other side.** ℰ

How is it that you Have No faith?

In the parable above, Jesus asked the questions, **"Why are you so fearful?"** and **"How is it that you have no faith?"** Have you ever had someone in your life look at you like, "You don't trust me nor do you have faith in me," I'm your father, mother, husband, brother…why don't you believe me?" Well, we know there are many reasons to the issues in life that can cause our heart to not trust and believe in others. But Jesus is our Savior and our Redeemer, and He said that He will "never leave us nor forsake us." However, many still find it hard to trust in Him!

Regardless of the storms that rage in our lives, when we have given ourselves in fellowship with Him by seeking His word and His presence, His love engulfs our weary souls and His peace calms the billowing seas of its rage.

An Interrupted Bulletin from the Lord!

When there are no thoughts of personal ambition or achievement and you are fully yielded to Me, I delight in you and take pleasure in serving you in order to take you to the other side, as I said I would do. I give to you, opportunities because I love you. The dream that I gave to you is my gift to you, so I know how to prepare and shape you to be ready to receive it. Jesus

Give Me an Opportunity

An Interrupted Bulletin from the Lord!

Give Me an opportunity in the opportunity that I've given to you! Let Me have a chance to reveal to you what occupies the dream that I have positioned in your spirit. Seize each moment that I bring along your pathway.

"And therefore the Lord [earnestly] waits [expecting, looking and longing] to be gracious to you; and therefore, He lifts himself up, that He may have mercy on you and show Loving kindness to you. For the Lord is a God of justice." (Isaiah 30:18 AMP)

God expresses His love through dreams, visions and opportunities to fulfill your desires.

An Interrupted Bulletin from the Lord!

Let me show you the depth of My Love by giving to you My heart for your life. Step out and take advantage of the opportunities. Trust Me for I trust you with My dream for My kingdom to be completed through you. You are my vessel. Jesus

       ဆ Give Me an opportunity in the opportunity that I've given to you! ဆ

Alternating Steps

. . . .

"And let us not grow weary while doing good, for in due season we shall reap if we do not lose heart." (Galatians 6:9)

In this chapter we will see that we must accomplish certain steps for Jesus to make His next move. When God gives to us an opportunity, the next step is ours. What we do with this moment is what God will do next in the process. But the enemy tries his best to destroy all that God has for us through constant weariness. When feelings of the flesh present reasons to give up and faint, dreams and visions will be aborted. However, God gives us three keys to the solution of our frustration and impatience along this journey. These keys unlock the accomplishment for the verses that require us to "do" something in the journey.

The first key from Galatian 6:9 is **"do not grow weary..."** Have you ever stopped to think what growing weary is? Looking up the word *weary* in the Webster's Dictionary; I found the meaning to be *physically or mentally exhausted; fatigued; tired; impatient and/or dissatisfied.* Wow! We can all relate to this word. It's easy to allow yourself to get in this position to become weary in the middle of an opportunity or assignment. As we draw near the end of the preparation, testing, and training for this opportune time, the final polishing to our character is refined by patience. This waiting period arrives causing us to feel as if Jesus has abandoned us and left us sitting on the shelf. Satan thinks that this is his time to attack our mind and start to convince us of lies, trickery and manipulation... which have been brewing within the hearts of our most loved and best cheerleaders, so we think. Because of these un-Godly thoughts, the enemy has beat down the smallest of faith within us. As we become frustrated and tired of believing the possible untrue words, throwing up our hands and walking away seems like a good thing to do!

This is exactly what Satan would love to see happen. Our walking away from this blessing would be the enemy's way to destroy God's assignment for His Kingdom purposes. But this key is telling us ***not*** to become weary! So how do we avoid becoming impatient, frustrated, tired, dissatisfied, exhausted and fatigued? When God spoke that word in your heart in the beginning, it was fiery, but now it seems to have become stagnated, stale and maybe untrue. Doubt has started to wrap itself deeper in the deceptive lies. Now your heart is hardened by disappointment and discouragement with little determination left. Your belief and faith weaken daily. Have you ever felt like that? Are you in that place now? If so, hold on, there's more to come. Let's go to the second key.

℘ *When God gives to us an opportunity, the next move is ours.* ℘

The second key of this verse tells us to **"keep on doing good,"** so don't stop blessing others and walking in His ways. Continue to open the door for that little old lady or tell someone that Jesus loves them. Remember, the number of opportunities that are given to us during a day are numerous. Don't withhold goodness from others just because God is taking you through a long and waiting process that will develop you for the dreams you hold. You may be the only Jesus they ever see. Feeding the hungry and blessing the poor are specific instructions from Jesus. Learning to give good gifts comes from a heart of love, and we reap what we sow. As we continue to bless others, we must continue to be open to receive from Jesus in areas for our growth. Therefore, seize each moment wisely for the Lord.

The third key that is mentioned in this verse is **"do not lose heart."** After growing weary how can you not "lose heart" over the things that you were hoping for? Let's face it, discouragement can come easily, causing us to lose our enthusiasm and our heart of purpose. Then throwing our hands up and walking away sounds good. And as I said, Satan would love to see that happen.

The word *lose,* from Webster's Dictionary, means *to come to be without; to get rid of; to forfeit the possession of; leave behind; to suffer defeat; to fail to gain or win.* When we meditate on the issues at hand and assume God has walked away from His promise to us, hope is deferred or lost. We "feel" defeated, dried up with no spunk left within; therefore, our dreams and visions of blessings will be delayed for another time. Repeating a phrase spoken in another chapter, which is worth tucking under your skin is: **"Delays are not denials."**

"...vs 15 And so it was that he [Abraham], having waited long and endured patiently, realized and obtained [in the birth of Isaac as a pledge of what was to come] what God had promised him." (Hebrews 6:13-15)

After Abraham patiently endured, he obtained the promise. Boy that hits the nail on the head! Our promises have not been abolished, just delayed. When the Lord received your request to become Lord of your life, He gave His Word to prepare you for your destiny. These two start-up verses, *"Don't despise the day of small beginnings"* and *"His ways are not our ways"* help us to Know that the journey may start long and small and He's going to do things His way. When we step ahead of Him, we can cause disastrous things to happen and prolong the next step from occurring in the proper time. With these encouraging words and others, learning how to pray for those in the connection set-up can help prevent setbacks for both receivers in the journey. However, praying, walking in patience and joy and expecting things to occur in His timing can also become the devil's playground. The enemy sees this period of your life "empty" as to what you're seeking. Wanting you to lose heart and give up by becoming weary and impatient, he starts to fill your mind with negative and lying thoughts. But your spiritual weapon is to keep doing good and not give up! The enemy never likes it when you challenge his arrows with the Word of God! The Lord desires to see your destiny fulfilled as much as you do. But we must realize that the keys we are given are to be used and walked out before His next move is appropriate. This step depends on your determination to finish the race.

ℴ *"Delays are not denials."* ℴ

It would be to our advantage not to lose heart at what is happening on the forefront. **Know** that Jesus is working behind the scenes for your destiny to be fulfilled.

Ok, now that you've applied the three keys to your move…Oops, forgot the keys…what were they again? Galatians 6:9 -- the three keys that are required in your move are:

1. Do not grow weary
2. Keep on doing good
3. Do not lose heart

So, what are the "to do's" that develop our character? Every time we make choices, we are developing our character. Every time we "do not grow weary," "keep on doing good," and "do not lose heart" we are making choices to "do."

ℴ *Thoughts determine what you want,*
Actions determine what you get. ℴ

To Do's

Let's take the first key, **"Do not grow weary."** Look at this verse from the Word.

"When Gideon came to the Jordan, he and the three hundred men who were with him crossed over, exhausted but still in pursuit." (Judges 8:4 NKJV)

Have you ever been so tired and exhausted that you were about to drop, faint, had to sit down or just stop and rest? Imagine these men with Gideon fighting the enemy when they were exhausted. They kept pushing forward to complete the task regardless of how they felt. During this journey of preparation for the opportunity we have been given, we must have the same determination as they did: pushing forward even when we're tired and weary from working, ministry, counseling, etc. The goal is before us and whatever it takes to get there, we must do it.

The Word has filled our hearts with encouragement and direction when those times come. David cries out in Psalm 6:2 saying, *"Have mercy on me for I am weak, and my bones are troubled."* We are told in Isaiah 40:29, 31 that He gives power to the weak with verse 31 saying *"if we wait upon the Lord that He'll renew our strength where we will mount up with wings like eagles and run and not be weary and walk and not faint."* So, encouraging words from the Lord are at our fingertips.

God's Word provides us invigorating and supportive help in life, and a good example of His uplifting words for when we're weary and feel defeated is in this verse:

"Come to me all ye who labor and are heavy laden, and I will give you rest." (Matthew 11:28 NKJV)

The enemy loves to find a person who is emotionally and physically exhausted. When he finds a person with these symptoms of tiredness, being worn out, exhaustion, sleepiness, etc., he likes to think he has freedom to attack. Look what Ahithophel said to David's son, Absalom:

"I will come upon him while he is weary and weak and make him afraid. And all the people who are with him will flee, and I will strike only the King." (2 Samuel 17:2 NKJ)

1 Peter 5:8 says that we must *"Be sober, be vigilant because your adversary the devil walks about like a roaring lion, seeking whom he may devour."* The enemy waited for David to become weak and weary before he attacked, and he operates in the same manner today. He waits for this moment in your walk and journey to attack you until he wins. That's why not growing weary is an important key in our journey of "to do's."

Now the second key that requires for us to "do" something is **"Keep on doing good."**

The perfect way to define "good" is "obedience." When we obey, we're being good by walking in goodness, speaking and acting in love and caregiving to those in need, etc. God spoke about goodness as obedience in Deuteronomy 28:1-2; 15. The blessings are received when we obey, and the curses come when we disobey. But during the bootcamp of training for our assignment, our flesh may be unwilling to be submissive. It can be hard and frustrating to walk in goodness when we feel like throwing in the towel. But Praise God, it is possible.

When we have a heart to obey because we love Him, God will reward. Matthew 26:6-13 says that the woman with the alabaster box poured expensive perfume on the feet of Jesus. Then she wiped His feet dry with her hair. This was an act of goodness from her heart. Ephesians 5:1 tells us to imitate Him as beloved children. Walking in the ways of God causes us to walk in a likeness of Him who is good. Therefore, to be good is to ardently maintain our life in His ways. Psalms chapter 1 says that if our delight is in the Lord and we meditate on Him day and night, we shall be stable and established like a tree planted by the rivers of water. And because you are connected to your water supply, you will bear much fruit *in its season*. John 15:5 reiterates the same concept. By staying connected to Jesus, the vine, we will bear much fruit. Goodness by obedience is a fruit of Christ and can produce more fruit.

"Set your mind on things above and not on things on the earth. (Colossians 3:2)

When we're earthly minded, we're no heavenly good. In the world today it's easy to get fearful, with our eyes focused on the chaos. Therefore, our minds should be set on the things above and not here on this earth. Don't get me wrong; we need to pay attention, be alert and aware of what is happening, but in the midst of these troublesome times, God's Love casts out fear. It's our responsibility to continue to obey His commandments in His Word. The book of Timothy tells us that in the last days Christians will be deceived and fall away. We are in a crucial time where we must listen to God and pay attention to what His word is saying. Do not be weary in doing good, and most of all, do not lose heart. So, as we stay connected in fellowship, reading the Word with Praise and Worship, the Blood of Jesus will protect and shield us from the enemy's attacks. Remember, the enemy is roaming about looking for the crack in the shield to enter and deceive.

The third "to do" is **"Do not lose heart."**

"Be anxious for nothing, but in everything by prayer and supplication, with thanksgiving, let your request be made known to God." (Philippians 4:6)

Yes, we're all anxious to finally complete the journey of our destination in this opportunity; however, there are strings attached to the contract. It is an honor to have a Father who cares to protect us from the enemy's deceitful ways of destruction. Preparing us and making sure we are solid with deep roots of stability before we tackle the request of this assignment, His words may seem tough to hear and hard to swallow.

In First John, the Christians in Ephesus had lost their first love. New doctrines were entering the church and the true basics of Christianity were fading away. John's assignment was to bring these Christians back to the reality of the truth. The message he preached stirred within and was tough to swallow and hard to receive. Why? The word used for their behavior was not a sweet pat on the back. However, these words were spoken to stir within their hearts the status of their relationship with God and to warn them of the deception of the enemy. Damaging storms are developed to break the Christian down, devastating their dreams and vision to where they lose heart in their destiny. Let's look at a few verses in Chapter 1 and Chapter 2 of 1 John.

"If we say that we have fellowship with Him and walk in darkness, we **LIE** and do not practice the truth." (1 John 1:6)

"If we say that we have not sinned, we call Him a **LIAR**, and the Word is not in us." (1 John 1:10)

"He who says I Know Him and does not keep His commandments, is a **LIAR**, and the truth is not in Him." (1 John 2:4)

"He who says that he is in the light, and hates his brother, is in **DARKNESS**." (1 John 2:9)

John's message was a striking sword leaving them no room to run. They were caught red-handed and without excuse. When the enemy tries to discourage us, God's word is there for us to examine our heart and relationship with Him. So, don't lose heart! Know that the Holy Spirit will bring to you the Word that will guide you back to the truth.

In Due Season

The middle phrase in Galatians 6:9 is, **"...for in due season we shall reap..."** This phrase is an incentive to the three keys we just examined. When we start to fulfill the obligation of these three points, harvest will come in its due season. Ecclesiastes chapter 3 shares that everything has a season and there's a time for every purpose; therefore, the finality of our journey has a special due date.

"In this you greatly rejoice, though now for a little while, if need be, you have been grieved by various trails, that the genuineness of your faith, being much more precious than gold that perishes, though it is tested by fire, may be found to praise, honor, and glory at the revelation of Jesus Christ..." (Peter 1:6-7)

"My brethren, count it all joy when you fall into various trials, knowing that the testing of your faith produces patience. But let patience have its perfect work, that you may be perfect and complete, lacking in nothing." (James 1: 2-4)

These two verses explain why delays seem to happen. Various trials start to resurrect the old man to the surface. And the mirror reflects an unknown identity when we discover who we are. Questions bombard our mind with unbelieving character of self. (No...that can't be me!!!!) Trusting that God has a reason for these trials, creating patience, developing faith, growing spiritual muscles to stand strong, and pruning, molding, reshaping our character, are necessary to become the image of Him! Therefore, we should be full of joy when we encounter these various trials. But when you don't know what to do, just stand. Be still, quite and wait for the Lord to present the next move.

"...and having done all, to stand." (Ephesians 6:13)

Our promotion day has a special due date and season. Glancing back at Galatians 6:9, we discussed three keys that require "doing" something. The testing of these times and other various trials will determine when our promotion day arrives. If the tests were not passed, God will always give us another chance. (Refer to Chapter 3)

His plans + obedience = Promotion
Let's look at another important step of this journey.

Behold... Listen

"Behold, the former things have come to pass." And new things I declare; Before they spring forth, I tell you of them." (Isaiah 42:9)

Frances J. Roberts in her book *Seize Each Moment* indicates that each moment is available to capture. However, there is one word that is camouflaged before taken into custody or seized. That word is *Listen*.

In the verse above, Isaiah 42:9, the phrase *spring forth* is used. The Webster Dictionary shows its meaning as "to leap out." When we are not expecting a surprise, something may jump out in front of us. It is unexpected and being unsure, we may walk away, run from it or even call for help. This verse prepares us for these "uncalled-for" visits. Seeing the old things passing away in our journey, God is implementing new things. But unless we know to listen for His voice, the announcement that He is doing a new thing may be overlooked.

Isaiah 48:3, repeats the message that God gives us in Chapters 42 and 43. *"I have declared the former things from the beginning; They went forth from My mouth, and I caused them to hear it,"* and these words came to pass. The words *"He caused them to hear"* should stir the heart of every reader. Why? The cause for hearing was not on an involuntary response. They were made to hear. But in verses 7 and 8, we are informed that they heard but *their ears were not opened,* implying that they never heard at all.

When God was training Samuel in his first prophecy, Samuel leaped from his sleep several times. He heard a voice speaking his name, so he jumped from his bed and ran to Eli, assuming it was him, but finally realizing that it was the voice of God speaking to him. Then the Lord said to Samuel:

*"Behold, I will do something in Israel at which both ears of **everyone who hears** it will tingle."* (1 Samuel 3:11) The ones who hear are those who are listening.

In the beginning when Jesus spoke the word for opportunity, our antennae must have been turned to the on position. Listening to His voice sparked an excitement to leap at this opportune time. Congratulations, we made it this far! But each step requires both ears to be open to hear. As the journey develops, the enemy stands on the side lines to put a roadblock up to prevent His voice of direction from being heard. Knowing this should cause us to always be alert and aware of what Christ is doing in our life. Many opportunities have slipped by our ear gates because of our not listening to Him. Taking that leap of faith in expecting to hear from Christ causes us to listen to the voice we hear inside. Just like Samuel. Even if we reach out in the wrong direction, the Holy Spirit will direct us back on course.

Little by little, as we obey each step, He will announce His next move with new directions. These moments are crucial. They require us to listen closely and obey, sometimes with a quick response. That's why listening closely is necessary. That opportune time may only be for that moment. So, the moment of obedience will bring forth the next step in this journey. Again, if you fail to hear or respond at that time, Jesus is gracious to give us the step again.

Chapter 13

Summary

. . . .

Throughout this book, we have seen how the Lord gives us direction and guidance in the dreams and visions that He places in our hearts. God has given us model examples of the Old Testament men. Seizing that moment of opportunity when an understanding and vision of the results were not clear, increased their faith in the Lord. Trusting that the Lord had a purpose in these favorable times, these men were used by God to give a demonstration of how the miracles of God set the stage for His Word to be written for generations to come. Realizing that the Old Testament is the New Testament concealed and the New Testament is the Old Testament revealed brings a hope of expectancy of knowing all things are possible, for God is the same today as He was yesterday, He never changes. What He did then, He can and will do now.

"...as His divine power has given to us all things that pertain to life and godliness, through the knowledge of Him who called us by glory and virtue, by which have been given to us exceedingly great and precious promises, that through these you may be partakers of the divine nature, having escaped the corruption that is in the world through lust." (2 Peter 1:3-4)

As opportunities are offered to us, God will provide all that we need in our journey. However, there are several keys that must be implemented. Developing these skills with character while birthing the opportunity that Jesus placed in your heart is an honor to receive. When I was a baby Christian, years ago, several Christian friends would share with me these words, which I mentioned in an earlier chapter. ***"Gifts can't take you where character can."*** If a cake comes out of the oven too soon, it will not be fully cooked and ready to eat. The same applies to us. The Word tells us not to despise the day of small beginnings; therefore, Christ takes precautions making sure we are prepared to be launched. It is His vision and plan, presented to us as an opportunity to complete. As we allow Christ to develop and prefect His character within us, testing times and trials will come. However, as the Word says, count it all joy, knowing these times will produce the fruit of God.

Fear may attempt to abort the step out of the boat. However, when we take a chance to seize that moment and then start the journey, we stand on what matters rather than what we know and see. Although the Biblical characters in this book were not aware of the Scriptures we know, they walked in them and believed in them. Refusing to give up, they stood on what they knew was important to Father God. Many oppositions faced them; however, they knew if God said they were going to the other side, they were going to the other side. Having an ear to hear and a desire to listen enticed them to complete their calling. Therefore, whatever battle we face, the answer is in the Word of God. As we have been Blessed with the Promises of God and the Word as our Sword, we have no excuse not to receive ALL that God has for us.

Not only is the opportunity for your destiny and purpose, but it's also to be a part of the "connection set-up" that will touch the lives of others around you. By choosing to take a *chance* and go in the opposite direction of where God is leading you, you may cause the opportunity that someone else may have had to accept Christ or to further their step toward their destiny to be aborted. And for you…well, your destiny steps will be delayed until you step back on the right path of obeying God.

I want to share one last example with you that I believe will be an encouragement for you.

When I was younger, I was a dedicated runner, and I played racquetball along with other sports that I enjoyed in my active days. When I was just starting to make running a hobby and a habit, I started out slow. I was running in an inside gym with four laps making a mile. I could barely make one completed lap without having to stop, but I had a goal set for each day. Each time I would increase my run by a half a lap until I finally graduated to four miles every other day. I was able to run five miles a couple of times, but I made myself sick. I knew my limit and that was four. But the point is I set a goal, and I wouldn't stop until I accomplished it. I knew each time what I could accomplish; therefore, I pressed forward toward that mark. In Christ we know that all things are possible. So why do we stop short of what we can do in Him when He has orchestrated the run?

"He who is in you is greater than he who is in the world." (1 John 4:4)

There's No excuse so don't give up!!!

Coat of Love

**"...For He has clothed me with the garments of salvation,
He has covered me with the robe of righteousness..."
Isaiah 61:10 NKJV**

Learning to walk a new walk is developed by learning a new Way when wrapped in the coat of His Love! Take advantage of the teachings that are available by checking out the itinerary of times and places along with the books that Papa has placed in my heart to share with you. For He will instruct you and teach you with His eye upon you; however, let these resources help develop the skills that have already been placed within you by the Creator that has created you for His kingdom while developing and building the character of Christ within. We will help you "put on" the Coat of Love that you'll never want to take off!

Books Available
Feared to Choose but Chose to Chance

Coat of Love Ministries
Shelia

Printed in the United States
By Bookmasters